THE LIBERATED CA[...]

A creative approach to canvas embroidery

Penny Cornell

M000273322

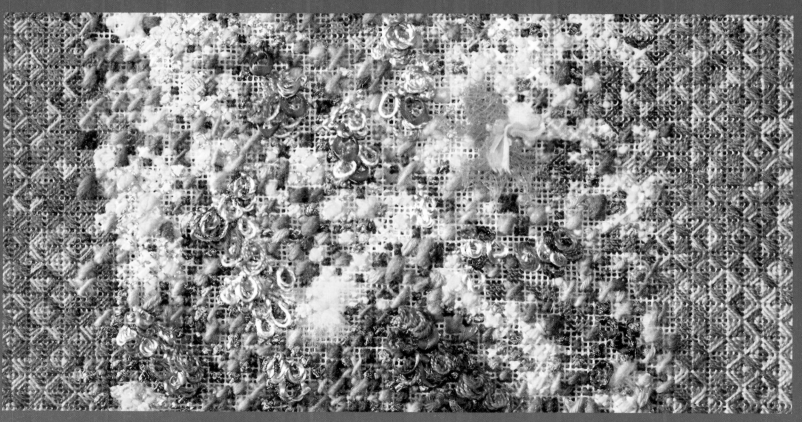

Published by Triple T Publishing c.c.
Cape Town

ISBN: 0-958 3873-5-4 ... Soft Cover edition
ISBN: 0-958 3873-4-6 ... Hard Cover edition

First Published 1995

PUBLISHED BY:
Triple T Publishing c.c.
29 Colenso Road
Claremont 7700
Cape Town, South Africa

Typesetting & Repro: Fotoplate, Cape Town
Printed by: Mills Litho, Cape Town

Text and illustrations by Penny Cornell.
Embroidered samples and pictures by Penny Cornell, unless otherwise stated.
Photographs on front cover and page 57 by Mike Carelse, and on page 5 by Pam Warne.
All other photographs and stitch diagrams by John Cornell.

Copyright © Penny Cornell 1995.

All rights reserved. No part of this publication may be reproduced, stored in a retrieval system or transmitted in any form
or by any means without the permission of the copyright holder. The use of photocopiers for copying or enlarging the
illustrations and sketches is permitted for personal use only. However, the sale or distribution of such copies is an
infringement of the copyright laws.

Acknowledgements

I should like to thank all those who have contributed to the production of this book, especially my husband, who for more years than I care to remember, nagged me to write a book on embroidery. I am grateful to him for the hours he spent patiently working out the stitch diagrams, taking hundreds of photographs and proof reading. Both he and my daughter Katrina-Jayne have always been active, honest and valued critics of my work: their patience and support are greatly appreciated. I am also indebted to my students and embroidery friends for their input, encouragement and inspiration, especially Maré Abbott, Tricia Elvin-Jensen, Jutta Farringer, Pam May, Toody Mouton, Jennie Stock, Luise Tyler and Gretchen Reich who allowed me to use their work. Thanks also to John Drew, Derek Gardner and Barrie and Jin Howard for permission to include pieces of my work which they now own, and to the South African Cultural History Museum for permission to use the photograph of the tapestry from the Le Jeune collection on page 5. I should also like to thank Edward Ralph for inventing the name of the "Bad French Knot". Finally I thank Lesley Turpin-Delport and Mike Tripp for their help, guidance and patience.

CONTENTS

Dedicated to my aunt, Doris Tice,
who introduced me to the wonders of embroidery
when I was a small child.

About the Author

Penny Cornell was born and grew up in England. She studied both embroidery and art at Hammersmith College in London. She came to South Africa to visit her parents for a holiday – and stayed on in Cape Town. There she met and later married her husband John, who was studying nuclear physics. Penny worked briefly as a designer in a badge factory, then changing direction she made a career for herself as a draughtswoman with a firm of civil engineers, drawing roads, bridges and freeways! She returned to England with her husband when he spent three years at Oxford doing post-doctoral research work, and Penny found employment with a firm of structural engineers until their return to Cape Town. However embroidery was never far from her mind, and she continued to design and produce commissioned works such as pulpit-falls for churches, a standard for the Chief Commissioner of the Girl Guides, embroidered pictures, and even decorative bead embroidery on angora jerseys.

Penny has held several exhibitions of her work, and has regularly exhibited with the Cape Embroiderers' Guild, of which she was a founder member and later Secretary. She continues to give courses in her home studio in many different aspects of embroidery, from traditional Blackwork and Canvas Work through to Creative Embroidery and Machine Embroidery. Penny has lectured for the University of Cape Town Summer and Winter Schools, and has also been invited by Guilds in other cities in South Africa to lecture and run workshops. She has written correspondence courses in Creative Embroidery and Canvas Embroidery for the Home Study College of South Africa, and tutored students following these courses. Her work has been exhibited in Japan – as part of the DMC Centenary Exhibition – and more recently in Maastricht, Holland. Penny is presently Chairman of the Cape Embroiderers' Guild. Penny also finds time to do housekeeping and look after her husband, daughter, a cat and three ducks.

An example of a finely woven antique tapestry, from the Le Jeune Collection in the S.A.
Cultural History Museum, Cape Town.
(Photograph by Pam Warne.)

INTRODUCTION

To many, the name *Canvas Embroidery* suggests *Tapestry* or *Needlepoint*. It would perhaps be appropriate at this point to define these terms. **Canvas Embroidery** is stitching worked on canvas or a canvas-like fabric. Early examples were worked in *Tent Stitch* and *Cross Stitch* often on very fine canvas, whereas a true **Tapestry** is woven on a loom warp with the weft beaten down so as to cover the warp threads completely. The tapestries made in mediaeval times were generally used as hangings or wall coverings. The warp threads were usually of a strong linen and the weft wool or silk; they were frequently woven sideways, which means that the warp runs horizontally when the tapestry is hung. **Needlepoint** is the name used by many to describe canvas embroidery today and tends to mean printed or charted designs worked mainly in *Tent Stitch,* although more recently, it includes designs which incorporate a greater variety of textured stitches.

When **Canvas Embroidery** or **Canvas Work** as it is often called, is mentioned people often think of its utilitarian uses, such as chair seats, cushions, stool tops and bags, maybe even belts and book covers. For all these uses it needs to be hard-wearing and durable. It will most probably be sat on or worn, so raised stitches, uneven textures or long stitches lying on the surface would not be practical.

If we consider using **Canvas Work** techniques for projects which do not need to be durable, then the possibilities for experimenting and trying a new approach are endless. Contrasting and raised textures become a feature of the work instead of something to be avoided.

We have been brought up to think that the canvas must always be completely and evenly covered. But if you are making a picture or hanging this is not necessary. By using finer threads, such as stranded cotton, machine rayon and metallics, a delicate, almost ethereal effect can be achieved. By covering the canvas with a sheer fabric, areas can be left unstitched, in contrast to stitched or highly textured areas. The canvas can be coloured, cut, moulded, appliquéd, machine wrapped, or have things applied to it....

We are not restricted to conventional canvas work stitches either.

Stitches such as *Cretan Stitch* and *Backstitch Wheels* can be worked on canvas, and so can all the knotted stitches like *French, Bullion* and *Colonial Knots. Buttonhole Filling* can be used along with *Couching* and *Raised Chain Band. Needleweaving* can be worked on top of stitched or covered areas or to applied and padded areas, as well as over cut or withdrawn canvas, as in **Drawn Thread Work.** In fact, almost any stitch can be adapted for working on canvas. It is even possible to do **free machine embroidery** on canvas.

In order to try a new approach, one must first break free from preconceived ideas and open one's mind to all possibilities, in other words be prepared to experiment and to let the imagination have a free rein. This freedom to do as you please may not come easily at first, especially for those who have always been precise and counted their threads, or who like everything that they make to be 'useful'. But don't give up, allow your creative ability to grow and blossom, believe me it *is* there. It is just waiting to be released!

This book aims not only to provide some basic instruction, but to inspire you and show you the way towards creating your own designs. By studying the various stitch and experimental samples and reproducing them, or better still, attempting your own, you should soon gain the confidence to create larger pieces of **Liberated Canvas Embroidery.**

Someone (a non-embroiderer) once asked me what I called the type of embroidery that I do and I had to admit that none of the current terms, such as 'creative' or 'free-style' embroidery seem really right. She thought for a moment and said, 'How about "liberated" embroidery?'

I hope that with the help of this book, you may find much pleasure in creating your own "liberated canvas work"!

Right: An example of canvas work using a variety of stitches and worked in Persian yarn and pearl cotton (Coton Perlé) thread; a design like this one would be described by many as Needlepoint.

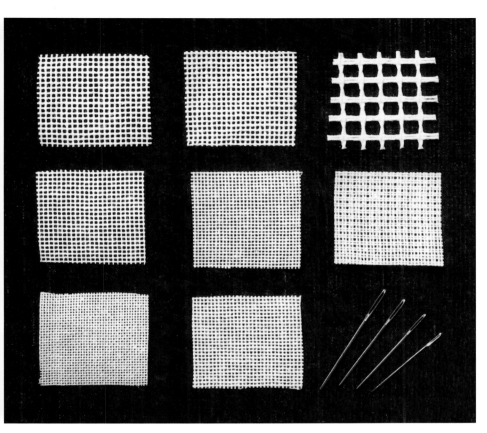

A selection of different gauges of Mono Canvasses, a piece of Rug Canvas (top right) and Double-Thread Canvas (centre right).

To work a simple piece of Canvas Embroidery you will need the following basic equipment:

- Tapestry needles in sizes ranging from 18 to 24
- A pair of embroidery scissors as well as some cutting out scissors for cutting the canvas
- A thimble

- A square embroidery frame or an old picture frame and drawing pins
- A piece of Mono Canvas
- A selection of threads
- Masking tape.

CHAPTER 1
Canvas and Equipment

CANVAS

There are two basic types of canvas which can be used for Canvas Embroidery. These are *single-thread* or *mono canvas,* and *double-thread* canvas which is sometimes also referred to as Penelope canvas.

Mono canvas, as the name suggests, is woven with single threads and is the most suitable for experimental work. The most stable is *interlock mono canvas* where the threads are twisted together and not just woven. *Double-thread* canvas is woven in pairs of threads: it is ideal for designs where cross stitch or petit point are required, and is usually used for pre-printed commercial designs.

Both single and double-thread canvasses are available in a variety of mesh sizes or *gauges*, the gauge being determined by the number of threads per 2.5 cm (i.e. per inch). The gauge can range from a very fine canvas of 32 threads per 2.5 cm up to a coarse canvas used for rug making, which may have as few as 4 threads per 2.5 cm. With double-thread canvas the gauge is determined by counting pairs of double threads per 2.5 cm. It is customary to refer to canvas as (say) 14 or 18 gauge single or double canvas.

Canvas can be bought in various widths as well as various gauges, so it is as well to check before purchasing to ensure that the canvas is *wide enough* to accommodate the planned piece of work. When buying canvas it is necessary to stipulate the amount required in metres, the width, the gauge and the type of canvas and, in some instances, the colour: for example one would ask for '1 metre of 68.5 cm (27 inch) 16-thread single interlock canvas in white.'

At first, the inexperienced embroiderer may be confused by the different gauges available, but you will soon develop a preference for a certain gauge, either from the appearance and delicacy of the required design or from the degree of ease with which you are able to see and count the threads. It is up to the embroiderer to choose which he or she prefers. However, as very different and interesting effects will result from using different gauges of canvas, it is a good idea to buy modest amounts of varying types and gauges rather than to purchase a whole metre of one type.

PREPARATION OF THE CANVAS

Before cutting the canvas and beginning to stitch, the canvas should be carefully measured to ensure that a margin of *at least* 5 cm (2") has been allowed *around the finished work*. It will need to have the edges bound and then be attached to the frame. By using a frame you will avoid any distortion of the canvas whilst work is in progress. This will do away with having to stretch it on completion. Working on a frame also allows stitches to be well formed and an even tension achieved.

Once the canvas has been cut, the 4 edges must be bound to avoid fraying and prevent the working thread from becoming caught and damaged in the rough edges of the canvas. Wherever possible, one should try to keep the selvedge of the canvas on the side of the work rather than at the top or bottom. To bind the edges, you can either use masking tape or fabric tape: the latter would need to be sewn onto the canvas.

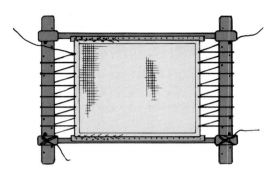

Embroidery Slate Frame showing canvas attached to the webbing on the rollers with Herringbone Stitch and laced with string to the side slats. The canvas would be attached to a Rotating Frame in a similar way.

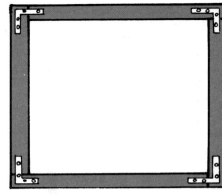

Home-made wooden frame assembled with angle brackets. The wood used for such a frame needs to be hard enough not to warp but soft enough to allow drawing pins to be pushed into it.

FRAMES

There are various frames available to the embroiderer. For canvas embroidery you will need a square or rectangular one. Putting canvas into a round embroidery hoop will damage and distort the canvas and should *not* be used unless the canvas is edged with sufficient fabric, such as calico. This allows the extra fabric to be mounted in the hoop, without damaging the canvas. Canvas can be attached to an old wooden picture frame (or a home-made frame) using drawing pins, if a proper frame is unavailable. Attach the canvas to the frame as shown in one of the diagrams making sure that it is stretched taut, but not distorted.

When working small experimental or stitch samples, I attach my canvas to a home-made plywood frame with masking tape. This little frame is only about 15 cm square, the centre having been cut out with a fretsaw.

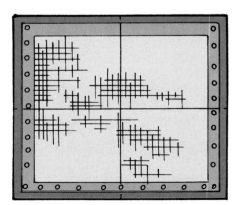

Home-made frame with canvas attached using drawing pins.

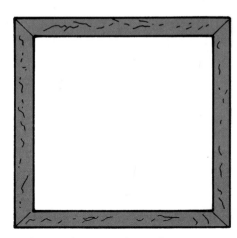

With a wooden picture frame, the canvas would be attached with a staple gun or drawing pins, as in the figure at left.

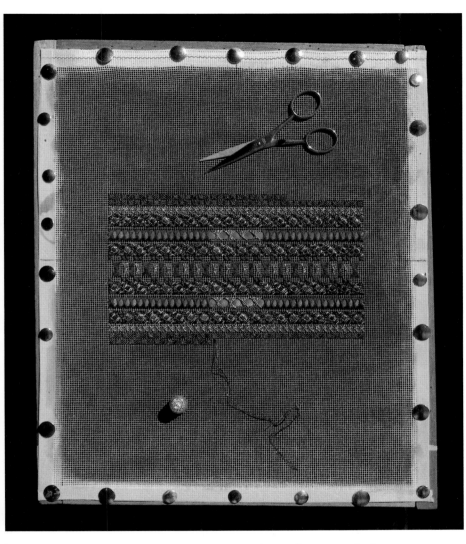

Ready to stitch: canvas mounted on a home-made frame.

BEGINNING TO STITCH

Owing to its stiffness, when working on canvas, stitches are worked in two movements of the needle. It is pushed UP through the hole, pulled to the other side, and then pushed DOWN through the next hole. Tightening of the thread is done from the right side of the work.

It is important not to work with too long a thread. Woollen threads will wear thin from continuously being pulled through the canvas: this causes them to become weak and break. Mercerised and silky threads loose their shine and knobbly threads are inclined to self-destruct! The ideal length is approximately 50 cm (19").

To begin working, make a knot at the end of your working thread and take the needle down from the front of the work to the underside, a short distance from the point where you wish to start stitching, leaving the knot on the right side of the work. This is called a waste knot, and provided you work towards the knot you will soon sew over the thread lying on the underside, thus securing it. When you reach the knot it can be snipped off, but do make sure that the thread has been sufficiently secured before removing the knot. When your working thread is finished, the end can be brought to the front of the work a short distance away from the last stitch worked. Once the threads on the underside have been caught and secured, the short lengths can be snipped off, in the same way as waste knots.

If your frame does not have a stand, it can be rested on the edge of a table so as to allow one hand to be below the frame and the other above. With practise this method will soon be mastered and will help to ensure an even tension in your work.

In many instances it will not be necessary to mark a design onto your canvas before stitching; stitch samples and experiments can be worked directly onto the canvas. Some designs are worked from a drawing on graph paper, others are painted using fabric or transfer paints; these methods are dealt with in chapter 3. However if you do wish to draw on your canvas, make sure that you use a waterproof pen or marker. Do not use a dark colour, especially if working with pale coloured threads or yarns and keep all marks to an absolute minimum. You may wish to leave an area unstitched but find you can't because an unsightly line is still visible! A hard pencil (3H) may be used, but beware of graphite rubbing off onto your threads as you work.

USEFUL POINTS ON WHICH TO PONDER:

1. Mark the centre of the webbing on the rollers (the end pieces) of your frame with a permanent marker so as to avoid having to measure each time you use the frame.

2. Never work in bad light. If the overhead lighting is poor, arrange to sit under an 'angle-poise' lamp or a strong reading lamp. If you have to struggle to see what you are doing you will lose interest and get little enjoyment from the work. The use of a blue 'daylight' bulb is advisable.

3. When working on a frame, it is a good idea to rest the frame either on the backs of two dining chairs or on a table. Then sit with the other end of the frame at chest level. To prevent the frame from slipping, if rested on a table, anchor it with a heavy book or covered brick.

4. Whenever possible work with your back well supported. ONE IS INCLINED TO HUNCH THE SHOULDERS AND LEAN FORWARD, especially when concentrating on something new; this causes backache and even headaches. A straight-backed chair with no arms is ideal. Do relax the neck and shoulder muscles every so often and get up and move around at least once an hour. It is a good idea to stretch your neck and rotate your head in a circular movement, first one way and then the other. Try stretching each arm, alternately, vertically up towards the sky about four times: this releases tension in the neck and shoulder. Another good exercise is to rest one hand on a table, lean forward and allow the other arm to hang loosely from the shoulder, then gently swing the arm backwards and forwards: this keeps the shoulder joint supple.

5. When threading wool through a needle, fold the end around the needle to form a 'U' shape, slide it off the needle and squeeze the 'U' together; this should then slide easily through the eye of the needle. If the end of the thread is fluffy, or uneven cut it off. Avoid licking the thread when inserting it through the needle. When working with knitting ribbons you may find that they have a tendency to unravel: should this occur, snip off the end immediately to avoid loss or waste.

6. When cutting yarn and threading it through the needle, the end furthest from the skein, ball or reel, is the end which goes through the needle. This practise ensures that the original twist of the thread is maintained. If a thread becomes over twisted allow it to dangle down and unwind. If it becomes untwisted then two or three twists in the right direction should restore its condition. If it does not, end off and take a new length of thread.

7. Remember that when placing stitches and designs onto the canvas that you are counting THREADS not holes!

8. Relax, enjoy yourself and be creative!

A piece of free Florentine work. (*By Jutta Farringer.*)

CHAPTER 2
Useful Stitches

There are many stitches which can be used on canvas – those designed for canvas or counted thread embroidery as well as those surface stitches not normally associated with canvas embroidery. Some lend themselves to experimentation more successfully than others and it is a great challenge to find new variations and effects. The stitches featured in this book should not be considered the ultimate selection, they are intended as a guide and a means of preliminary inspiration.

STITCHES FOR EXPERIMENTAL WORK

Canvas Work stitches

- ❏ Tent Stitch
- ❏ Half Cross Stitch
- ❏ Cross Stitch
- ❏ Cushion Stitch
- ❏ Crossed Cushion Stitch
- ❏ Rhodes Stitch and variations
- ❏ Norwich Stitch
- ❏ Brighton Stitch
- ❏ Rice Stitch
- ❏ Wheatsheaf Stitch
- ❏ Smyrna Stitch
- ❏ Eyelet Stitch
- ❏ Velvet Stitch
- ❏ Florentine Stitch
- ❏ Parisian Stitch
- ❏ Hungarian Stitch

Non-Canvas Work stitches

- ❏ Buttonhole Filling
- ❏ Needleweaving
- ❏ French Knot
- ❏ Bullion Knot
- ❏ Couching
- ❏ Cretan Stitch
- ❏ Raised Chain Band
- ❏ Back Stitch Wheel
- ❏ Woven Picots

Don't be afraid to use a chenille needle, instead of a tapestry needle, when working composite stitches such as large Rice Stitch; especially when using braid or knitting ribbon for the base cross. A sharp-pointed needle allows the working thread to be pulled through easily. This is important when working with metallic threads as they are easily damaged if forced through fabric or other threads. Remember also that no matter whether the needle is sharp or blunt, it must be large enough to carry the thread through the canvas without distorting the canvas or damaging the thread.

A good example of experimental stitchery. The full picture can be seen on page 62. *(By Jutta Farringer).*

CANVAS STITCHES

TENT

HALF CROSS

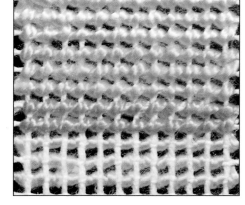

CROSS

TENT STITCH

Tent Stitch is the smallest stitch which can be worked on canvas. It is therefore invaluable for filling small areas and outlining. It can be confused with Half Cross Stitch, which from the front of the work looks the same. Tent Stitch is worked so that a long diagonal stitch forms on the reverse side of the work, whereas with Half Cross Stitch a straight vertical or horizontal stitch is produced. The bottom 3 rows of these two examples, have been worked from the reverse side. Tent Stitch is a stronger and fuller stitch, thus making it more suitable for items which will have a lot of wear. If a fairly large area is being covered it should be worked diagonally to avoid distortion of the canvas.

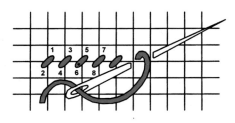

HALF CROSS STITCH

For creative work Half Cross Stitch is usually adequate and will use less thread, but do work either horizontally or vertically (not a mixture of both) especially when filling a fairly large area, otherwise unsightly ridges will occur.

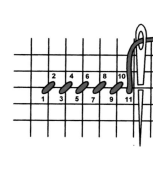

CROSS STITCH

Cross Stitch is usually worked over two threads of the canvas and can be worked one at a time or by working a row of half crosses first in one direction and then returning to work the second row in order to complete the cross. It is generally felt that for Canvas Work a stronger and more durable result is achieved by working the crosses individually. Cross Stitch, can of course, also be worked over any number of threads – horizontally and vertically – as can be seen in the picture *Summer Garden,* on page 60 which shows crosses of different sizes worked in a variety of threads.

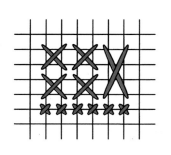

CUSHION AND CROSSED CUSHION STITCH

Cushion Stitch, or Satin Square as it is sometimes called, is a square stitch made up of diagonal stitches. The squares can be worked all in the same direction or reversed, to produce textured patterns as light catches the thread. They can be grouped in fours and the corners covered with additional diagonal stitches in contrasting types or colours of thread, thus forming Crossed Cushion Stitch. There are endless variations which can be achieved with this versatile stitch, especially if shiny and 'glitzy' threads are combined with matt or woollen ones. This is where the liberated concept really comes into play and allows the exploitation of unusual, daring colour schemes and combinations of thread.

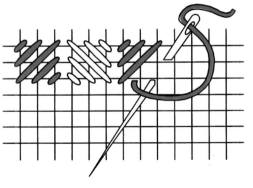

CUSHION

The top diagram shows Cushion Stitch worked in a row, over 1,2,3,2,1 diagonal threads of the canvas.

The picture (top right) shows Cushion Stitch worked in rows and forming squares. The green border has been worked in a variety of colours and types of thread to create greater depth and texture, and the canvas trimmed to follow the pattern formed by the stitches.

In the diagram (right) Cushion Stitch is worked over 1,2,3,4,3,2,1, diagonal threads of the canvas and arranged in a group of four. Cushion Stitch worked using a variety of threads and colours is shown in the picture (middle right).

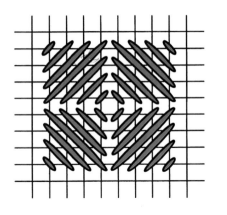

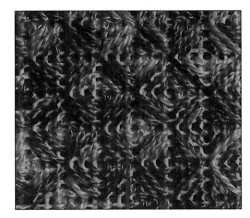

CUSHION in groups of four

The diagram (bottom) shows how Crossed Cushion Stitch can be formed by crossing the outer or inner corners of the Cushion Stitch.

In the picture (bottom right) Cushion stitch has been worked in stranded cotton and machine thread mixed together and then groups of four 'cushions' have been crossed to form patterns using gold thread.

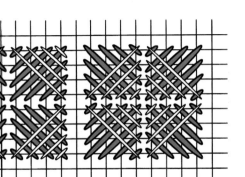

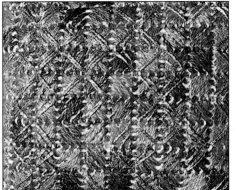

CROSSED CUSHION

**RHODES
starting
one thread
to right of
first corner**

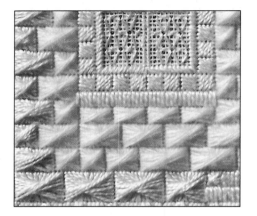

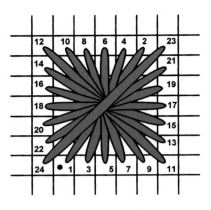

RHODES STITCH

This stitch can be worked over any number of threads, even or uneven, both as a square or an oblong. It can also be used to form fan-shaped patterns by working only half or a quarter of the stitch. Most books show Rhodes Stitch commencing at the bottom left-hand corner of the stitch and working from left to right around the square. It can also be worked by beginning one thread to the right of the bottom left-hand corner (see diagram top left) so that the final stitch travels from top right to bottom left, giving a crisper appearance to the finished stitch. To achieve other interesting effects it can be worked clockwise or anti-clockwise so as to capitalise on the light reflecting differently on this raised stitch. See examples on page 59.

RHODES STITCH – starting in the bottom left corner is shown in the middle diagram, and a stitched example is also given (left).

**RHODES
starting in
corner**

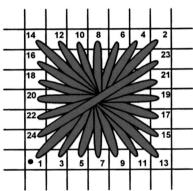

**HALF
RHODES**

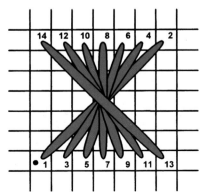

HALF RHODES STITCH

This stitch can also be worked from right to left or interlocked to form intricate patterns.

QUARTER RHODES STITCH OR FAN-SHAPED RHODES STITCH

If the last (vertical) stitch of the quarter Rhodes Stitch is omitted, the fan shape seems more pronounced, as can be seen at right. This also allows the stitch to be interlocked as shown.

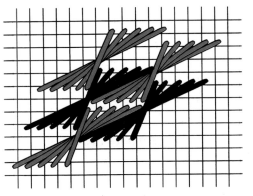

NORWICH STITCH – SOMETIMES KNOWN AS WAFFLE STITCH.

This interesting stitch is usually worked over an uneven number of threads (although it is possible to work it over an even number). The size of the stitch can be varied, as can be seen in the stitched example. Follow the order of the stitches carefully from the diagram and you will soon become familiar with the rhythm. Remember that the threads on the reverse side of the work do not at any time cross, but travel around the edge of the square. The last stitch which travels from 35 to 36 slips under the thread at 29 to complete the woven effect. If worked over an even number of threads the last 'round' of stitches will either need to share the centre hole, or this hole can be left vacant: both options work well. This stitch can be worked in thickish thread so that the canvas is covered completely, or in very fine rayon threads, as can be seen in the detail at the bottom of page 26. Some other interesting stitched examples can be found on page 35.

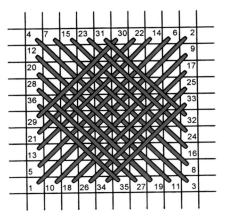

BRIGHTON STITCH

Brighton Stitch is really just a variation of Cushion Stitch, worked by placing the 'cushions' in groups of four, with the shortest diagonal stitches in the centre being replaced by a small vertical cross stitch, as shown in the diagram. See also picture on page 50.

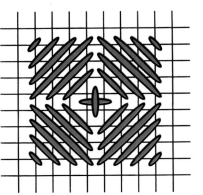

QUARTER RHODES

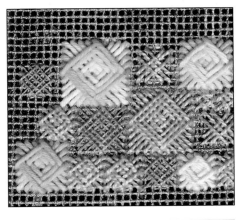

NORWICH

BRIGHTON

RICE

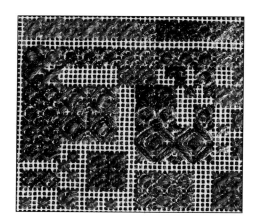

RICE worked over 8 threads

WHEATSHEAF

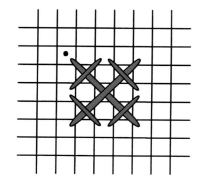

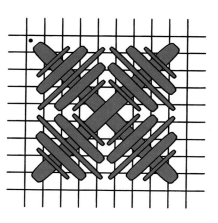

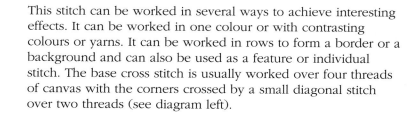

RICE STITCH OR CROSSED CORNERS

This stitch can be worked in several ways to achieve interesting effects. It can be worked in one colour or with contrasting colours or yarns. It can be worked in rows to form a border or a background and can also be used as a feature or individual stitch. The base cross stitch is usually worked over four threads of canvas with the corners crossed by a small diagonal stitch over two threads (see diagram left).

RICE STITCH WORKED OVER 8 THREADS OF CANVAS

The base cross can also be worked over six or eight (or even more) threads. This enables more diagonal stitches to be worked over the crosses. If different types and textures of thread are used a most exciting effect can be achieved. For example, the base cross can be a thick thread, a braid or knitting ribbon, so as to form a solid texture on which to work the finer contrasting threads. As we saw with Crossed Cushion Stitch, this is an ideal opportunity to experiment with colour and 'glitzy' threads. Further examples of Rice Stitch worked over 8 threads and used to create a background border or filled-in areas can be seen on pages 33, 51, 55 and 59.

WHEATSHEAF STITCH

Wheatsheaf Stitch is usually formed by working three vertical stitches over four or six horizontal threads of the canvas; these are tied together with a small horizontal stitch of any length, as shown in the diagram. But as can be seen in the stitched example (left), there is plenty of scope for experimentation. In the picture on page 49 the roof of the house was worked in a Wheatsheaf variation, while on page 59 there are examples where the stitch has been used in a variety of ways.

SMYRNA STITCH

This stitch is formed by first working an ordinary cross stitch over four threads of canvas, then placing an upright or vertical cross over it. It can be worked in rows as a background or as an individual feature stitch. It is a useful stitch to combine with Cross Stitch, Rhodes Stitch or Rice Stitch. A further stitched example can be found on page 50.

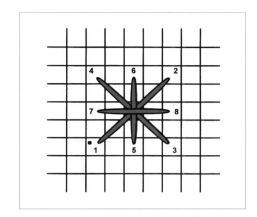

SMYRNA

EYELET

The diagram shows a square eyelet, but as can be seen in the stitched example (right), eyelets can be worked in an irregular fashion to form 'flowers', by varying the length and number of stitches. (Work either clockwise or anticlockwise, not randomly.) In the stitched example, different thicknesses, colours and types of thread were used and the spaces in between filled with Half Cross Stitch. This sample was worked whilst planning the *Dandelion Garden* which can be seen on page 50.

EYELET

VELVET STITCH

Velvet Stitch can be worked in rows or as an individual stitch. It is best to work from the bottom row up. If the loops are to be cut it is easier to do them all together once the area to be stitched has been completed. The stitched example shows Velvet Stitch worked in a variety of different threads, with the loops cut to form a pile as well as being left as loops. Further examples of this stitch can be seen on pages 42, 56 and 60.

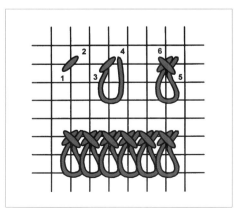

VELVET

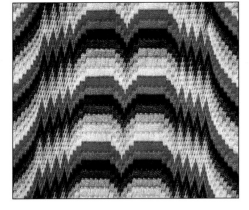

FLORENTINE

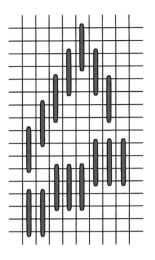

FLORENTINE STITCH

The name Florentine really describes a type of canvas embroidery rather than an actual stitch. It is characterised by the use of one straight vertical stitch which, by stepping it at regular intervals creates peaks, pinnacles and curved lines. The rather traditional patterns associated with Florentine Work can be incorporated into more free-style type of work by using unconventional threads and colour combinations, also by leaving areas unstitched. By following the stitch pattern, but using colours randomly, a most exciting effect can be achieved as illustrated on pages 10 and 43.

PARISIAN

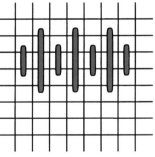

PARISIAN STITCH

This stitch is made up of vertical stitches over two and four horizontal threads of the canvas, worked alternately. With one type or colour of thread it results in an overall effect, but by using different colours and textures, stripes and patterns can be obtained. It is a very good background or filling stitch and forms a useful textural contrast to the raised, layered and woven stitches.

HUNGARIAN

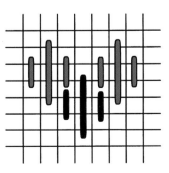

HUNGARIAN STITCH

This stitch is formed by working groups of three vertical stitches over two, four and two horizontal threads of the canvas, respectively, with one hole left open between the groups. The long stitch of each group fits into this hole on the next row, producing an interlocking effect. Like Parisian Stitch this is a useful filling stitch. See also the picture on page 50.

BUTTONHOLE FILLING OR DETACHED BUTTONHOLE

Buttonhole Filling is based on the fillings used in Needlelace. To begin, place a row of small vertical or horizontal stitches on the canvas and then work Buttonhole stitch through these stitches with the needle only going through to the reverse side of the canvas at the end of each row. The needle is brought to the front again below the first row, ready to commence another row. It depends how large a stitch is required as to how far below the previous row the next one is started. Rows of Buttonhole Stitch are worked back and forth, varying the size of the stitches and the tension to produce lacy effects. This can be worked over already stitched areas; it can be stuffed with fabric or threads or it can be worked over an area where the canvas has been removed – across the gap. It combines very well with Needleweaving. Wrapped wire shapes can be filled with Buttonhole Filling as well; this is discussed in Chapter 4.

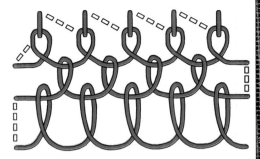
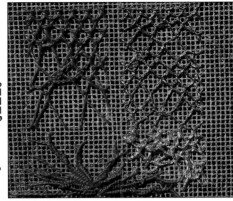

NEEDLEWEAVING

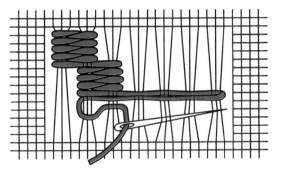

NEEDLEWEAVING

Needleweaving can be used on canvas in a variety of ways: worked directly onto the canvas as seen in the diagram (centre), or on top of an already worked area. It can be worked over portions of canvas where some of the threads have been withdrawn, as in Drawn Thread Work – see example (far right). A further excellent example of this can be seen in the flower picture to be found on page 47.

The stitch diagram shows needleweaving worked over the remaining threads of canvas, after some threads have been removed. To work it as in the example (right): place two or three long stitches onto the canvas and, beginning at the bottom, weave over these long stitches. Buttonhole Stitch can also be worked over part of the long stitches and combines well with Needleweaving.

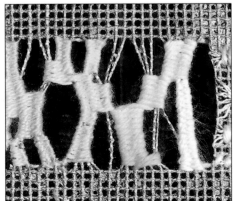

FRENCH KNOT

BULLION

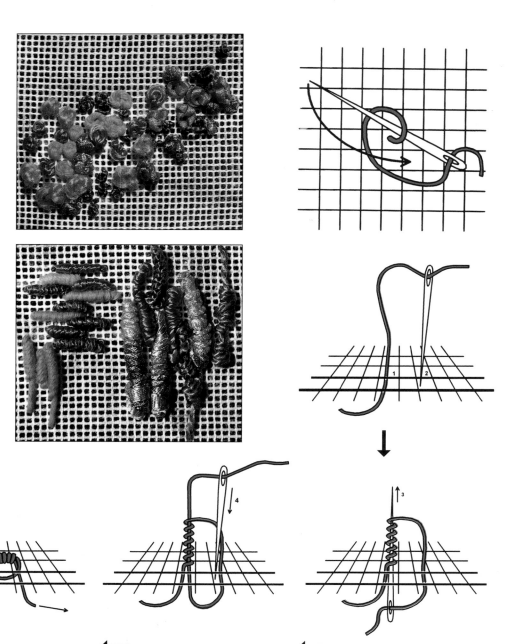

FRENCH KNOT

The French Knot is a wonderfully versatile stitch which can be worked directly onto the canvas or on top of an already stitched area as can be seen in the *Gilded Lily* on page 55.

The diagram shows the thread being wound around the needle once, before being taken through to the reverse side of the work. However it can also be wound around the needle two or three times to produce larger, fatter knots – but try not to do more than three turns as the knot becomes unstable. It is also as well to remember that knots made with a fine thread will disappear through the holes of the canvas. Traditionally French Knots are neat and firm, but a lovely effect can be achieved by working them loosely so that they form a loop – this is especially useful when making flowers. Ribbon and rayon threads work extremely well as they are springy. I was once explaining to a ten-year-old boy, who was working on a group project that I was organising, how to do these loose knots in a thick handspun yarn. After some thought he said, 'Oh! you mean you want me to do *bad* French Knots?'..... This type of knot has, ever since been known as a Bad French Knot by me and my students. Examples of both good and Bad French Knots can be seen in the *Knot Garden* on page 52.

BULLION KNOT

Bullion Knots can be made almost any length, they can lie flat or be made to form a loop or even have a tail. They look wonderful when climbing over each other. By using matt and shiny threads alongside each other, interesting textures can be achieved, as can be seen in the stitched example shown at the bottom of page 41. The diagrams at left show the method used for working Bullion Knots with the canvas or fabric on a frame.

COUCHING

Couching consists of a thread (often a very thick or knobbly one which will not easily go through the canvas) being laid onto the surface of canvas or fabric, with only the ends taken through to the reverse side of the work and secured. Another thread is used to stitch down the couched thread, this is traditionally a small vertical stitch placed at right angles to the couched thread at regular intervals. However these vertical stitches can be any length; they can be spaced or grouped to form patterns using any kind of contrasting texture or colour of thread as can be seen in the picture on page 53. Other stitches such as Cross Stitch or Wheatsheaf can also be used to hold the couched thread in place. Ribbon, braid or strips of fabric can be couched down in the same way.

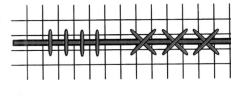

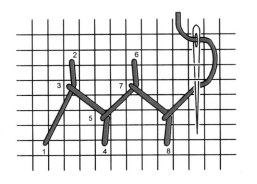

COUCHING

OPEN CRETAN STITCH

In the lower portion of the stitched example, Open Cretan stitch has been worked in a regular progression using a variety of threads and counting the canvas threads. Above this is an example of free stitching where no counting was done. The counted Cretan would form a very nice border, whereas the free Cretan could be used to fill a textured background area. It would also be very effective worked as a contrasting border to a very controlled piece of work.

OPEN CRETAN

RAISED CHAIN BAND

When this is worked as a normal surface stitch, it is necessary to work a ladder of horizontal stitches first, then work the chain over the ladder; however when working on canvas, especially if it is a coarse one such as rug canvas, the threads of the canvas can be used instead. In the stitched example the vertical threads of rug canvas were covered with zig-zag stitch using a sewing machine, then the raised chain was worked over the horizontal threads. It is of course not necessary to work over each horizontal thread, if a longer or varied stitch length is required. Remember not to pull the working thread too tightly as this will distort the raised, braided effect of the stitch. Raised Chain Band was worked in a knitting ribbon to form the inner border in the *Knot Garden* shown on page 52.

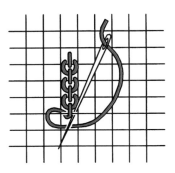

RAISED CHAIN BAND

BACK STITCH WHEEL

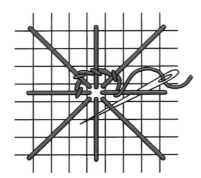

BACK STITCH WHEEL (WHIPPED SPIDER'S WEB)

Back Stitch Wheels are worked over an eyelet consisting of as many 'spokes' as are required. The needle is brought up in the centre of the eyelet and passed under two of the spokes; it is then passed back and around one thread and forward under the next, round the wheel until the spokes are completely covered; the needle is then taken through to the reverse side of the work. This stitch can also be worked over a largish bead so as to produce a raised 'sea urchin' effect, as in the border of *Maré's Knot Garden* shown on pages 3, 51 and 64.

WOVEN PICOT

WOVEN PICOT

Woven Picots can be made as long or as wide as required, or as is practical. The diagram illustrates the basic method of working, but it is important to make sure that the weaving is firm or the picots will look tatty. It is a good idea to push the woven threads down towards the point with the needle as you work. The longer the picot the more it will twist and curl when the pin holding the point is removed. Other stitched examples of Picots can be found on the cover and on pages 51 and 56.

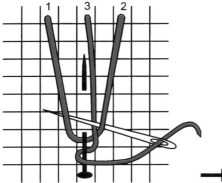 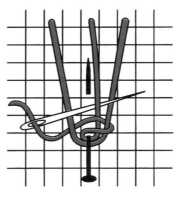

It is possible to begin the liberation process whilst learning and practising stitches. Once you have mastered the basic stitches try to work each one several times in at least three different thicknesses, textures and types of thread. Use different colour combinations – for example tones of one colour from dark to light, colours opposite each other on the colour wheel – to create dramatic effects; threads which change colour along their length, or several colours mixed together in the needle. Then vary the size of the stitches, or work only part of a stitch. Try working different stitches together, for example Rhodes and Cushion Stitch; Smyrna and Cross Stitch or Rice and Cushion Stitch.

CHAPTER 3
Changing the Canvas

There are a number of ways of changing the appearance of the basic canvas and therefore giving a greater freedom and experimental potential to the work.

OVERLAYS

Sheer fabrics such as silk, chiffon, or organdie can be used as covering overlays. Chiffon can be plain or printed: there are some wonderful floral prints available. Sheer fabric can be dyed using silk paints to obtain a mottled effect before applying to the canvas. An interesting effect can be achieved by laying silk or organdie on a stainless steel draining board and sponging paint onto the material. Then, while it is still wet, hang the fabric on a washing line and the paint will run down the fabric leaving lovely mottled effects. The organdie overlay in the picture *Misty* on page 53 was painted in this way. By placing these sheer fabrics over the canvas the effect of the threads is softened and this makes it visibly more acceptable to leave areas of canvas unstitched. This is also a way of colouring the canvas without actually painting it and gives a softer, more subtle appearance to the work. When stitching through a layer of fabric placed over the canvas it is important to make sure that the needle is pushed through the holes of the canvas *absolutely vertically* or the covering fabric will become distorted or puckered. It is also often advisable to use a sharp pointed needle instead of the normal tapestry needle.

PAINTING

Silk paint and fabric paint can be successfully used on canvas. It is advisable to have the canvas stretched onto a frame before applying the paint to avoid distortion when it becomes damp. Be sure to 'heat set' the paint or dye once it is dry. This is usually done by ironing on the reverse side, but a hair drier can also be used. One of the best ways to apply the rather thick fabric paints, especially the metallic ones, is to use the stiff nylon-bristled brush often found on the end of a dressmaker's marking pencil or a typewriter eraser: this allows the paint to be pushed into the canvas ensuring that it is well covered. Don't worry if some of the holes become clogged: you won't be stitching into all of them and some solid areas of paint can add to your design.

TRANSFER PAINTS

These can also be used, but they work best on canvas which contains a minimum of 'dressing'. Transfer paints are first applied, using a brush or sponge, to a non-absorbent paper (bond or photocopier paper is ideal) and allowed to dry. The painted paper is then laid face down onto the canvas and ironed with a hot iron until the image or design has been transferred onto the canvas or fabric. Bear in mind that the transferred image will be reversed! Remember to cover the ironing board with an old towel or sheet to avoid the colour being transferred where it is not needed through the holes of the canvas. It is a good idea to place a piece of embroidery fabric under the canvas, as the resulting by-product could be used for other projects. It is possible to place objects such as leaves, feathers, shapes or motifs cut from paper or felt etc., between the canvas and the painted paper to act as a resist. This leaves an uncoloured area on the canvas and by careful positioning of the resist, patterns and intricate designs can be printed.

SPRAY PAINT

Aerosol paints can be sprayed onto canvas – the metallic colours are particularly good. By placing stencils or cut out shapes, leaves or feathers onto the canvas as a resist before spraying, designs and patterns can be positioned ready for stitching. Remember to work in a well ventilated room when using aerosols, masking off areas which are not to be painted.

WATER-SOLUBLE PENCILS

These can be used to colour the canvas using the pencils to block in areas of colour. There are two ways of using these pencils: one is to rub the colour directly onto the dry canvas and then take a wet paint brush to spread and merge the colours; the other is to first wet the canvas and gently add the colour, again spreading with a brush or sponge to obtain the desired effect. The canvas should be stretched on a frame before painting. Take care not to make the canvas too wet and remember that – unlike the other methods mentioned – water-soluble pencils are *not* totally colour fast, although they need a fair bit of washing to remove completely.

For all the painting methods mentioned above, it is a good idea to experiment on small pieces of canvas to establish which is most suited to your needs. You will most probably develop a favourite and discard the rest. Remember it is always beneficial to investigate all the possibilities.

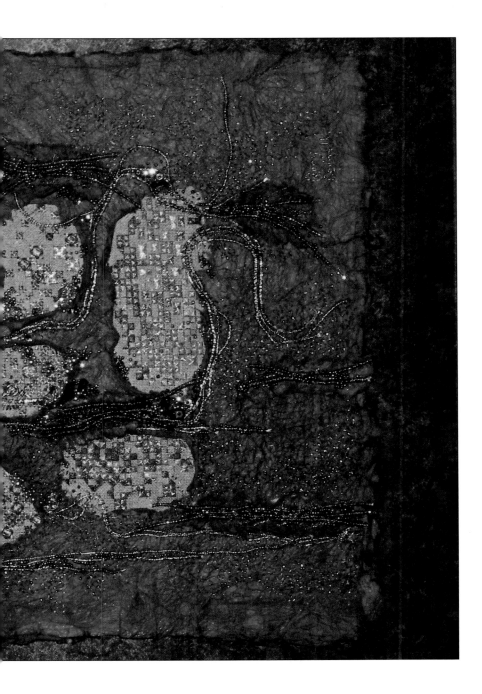

APPLIQUÉ

Areas of texture and colour can be added to the work by applying fabric, leather, lurex and glitter fabrics, stitched felt, or ruched ribbons, wrapped threads, braids or fabrics, and even pieces of knitting, tatting or crochet. Handmade paper, pieces of lichen, tree bark, or shells, as well as sequins, sequin waste, shisha and beads could be added to produce contrasts in texture. Some examples in which appliqué has been used can be found on pages 40, 55 and 58, as well as in the picture. *Mediaeval Fragments.*

JOINING DIFFERENT GAUGES

Interesting effects can be obtained by joining together pieces of canvas of different gauges – a good way to use up all the offcuts left over from other projects! Lay the pieces so that they overlap slightly and sew them together using your sewing machine set on zig-zag stitch. It is a good idea to colour the joined canvas, to help integrate the pieces before you start any further stitching. Choose stitches which can be worked successfully from one gauge to the other. Refer to the picture on page 62.

Mediaeval Fragments *(owned by Mr John Drew.)*

For this picture the canvas was first painted gold, and the stitching worked using fine rayon machine threads and a variety of gold threads. Handmade paper was then placed over the canvas, with holes torn in the paper to expose the stitched areas. Once the paper had been added to the canvas, pieces of gold thread were couched onto the sandwich using a sewing machine. Hand embellishment was later added using rayon, metallic threads and beads. The result is a very unusual presentation of canvas work.

OTHER WAYS TO CHANGE THE CANVAS

FREE-MACHINING

We do not immediately associate machine embroidery with canvas work, but it is possible to machine very successfully onto canvas. You can work ordinary zig-zag or Running Stitch on the canvas as you would for conventional sewing, but a better effect is achieved by setting the machine to do machine embroidery. To do this you will need to drop the feed-dog on your machine, or on some machines add a darning plate, remove the presser foot and set the stitch length to '0'. You will probably need to insert a larger needle than is used for normal sewing – size 90 or 100 and it will become blunt quite quickly so do not try to use it for other embroidery later: keep it for working on canvas. It will probably be necessary to adjust the top tension and remember to lower the presser foot lever before stitching.

The picture top right shows free Running Stitch and zig-zag worked on a piece of 18 gauge canvas. One big advantage of machining on canvas is that you can work without a hoop. The flowers in this sample were worked last of all, in Whip Stitch.

The border on the picture bottom right was worked in free Running Stitch over the organdie and canvas using a rayon machine thread, to form swirls suggesting leaves and a hedge. Loose, open Detached Chain Stitches and French Knots were added later to give more texture and strength to the hedge-like border.

The example on the opposite page was worked on a very soft linen canvas. Some threads were removed and with the machine set to 'free-machining' the remaining threads were pulled together and some were wrapped, using a zig-zag stitch. Later, canvas work stitches were added by hand.

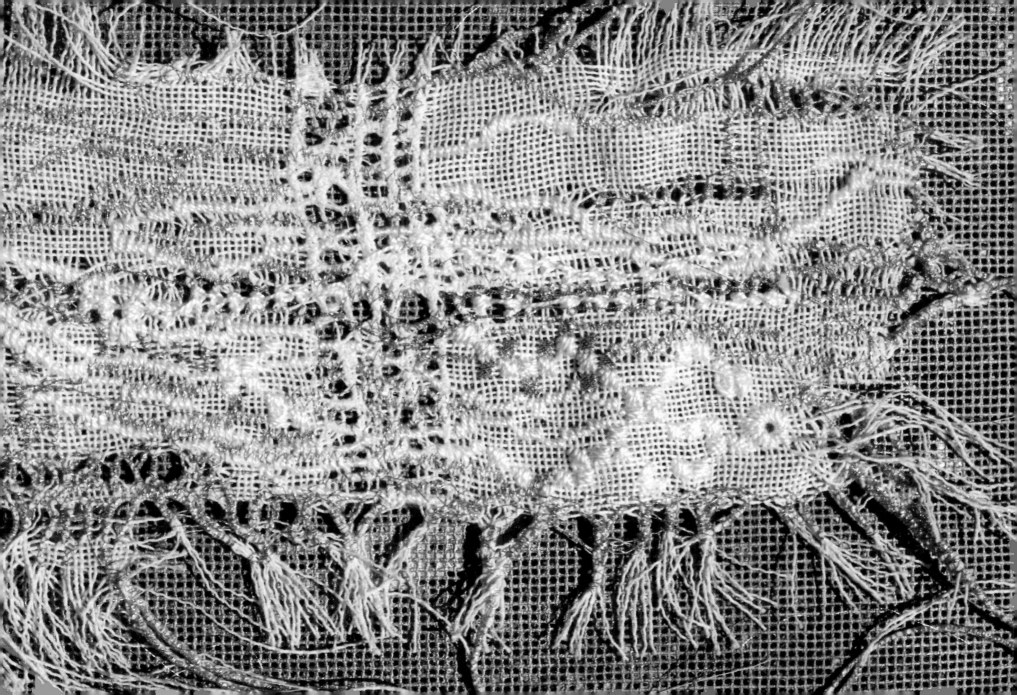

MACHINING ONTO RUG CANVAS

Any machine thread can be used to wrap the thick threads of rug canvas, but metallic threads look particularly good. The machine should be set for normal zig-zag or free-machining with the feed-dog lowered, whichever is preferred. By zig-zagging backwards and forwards over the threads, the canvas is covered to form a new base. Threads can be removed to create holes, as has been done in the example shown on the right.

Hand stitching can of course also be added: for example, needleweaving or wrapped string. If large areas of canvas are removed, machine stitching can be worked over the resulting gaps to produce a lacy effect.

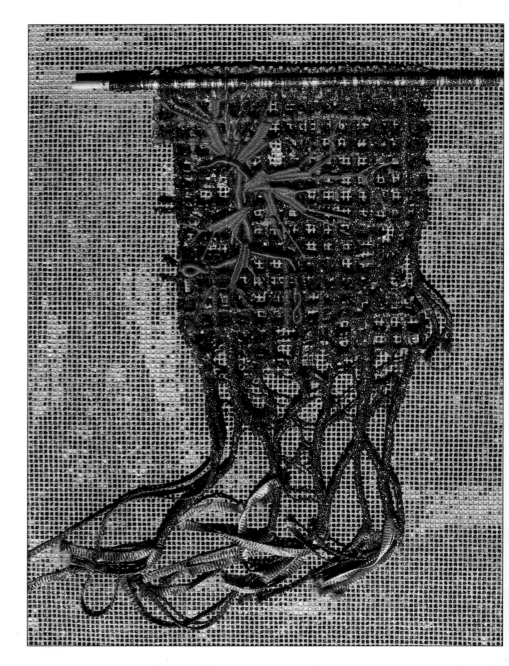

The picture on the right shows another example of machining on rug canvas. Some canvas threads were removed and machining was worked across the gaps. The fringe at the bottom was made by looping knitting ribbon onto the edge of the canvas and then machine-wrapping the ribbon. The rod at the top is a kebab stick, painted gold and then machine-wrapped – it *is* possible, if you run your machine *very* slowly! (In the photograph the sample is placed on a piece of gold-painted 18 gauge canvas.)

In the example on the opposite page the rug canvas was painted gold and then strips of fabric were woven through the threads of the canvas allowing some of the strips to loop or fray. Machine stitching was added to secure the fabric. This would form a wonderful base fabric for an evening bag or a border for a piece of work. Beads and surface stitchery could be added to achieve a really rich effect.

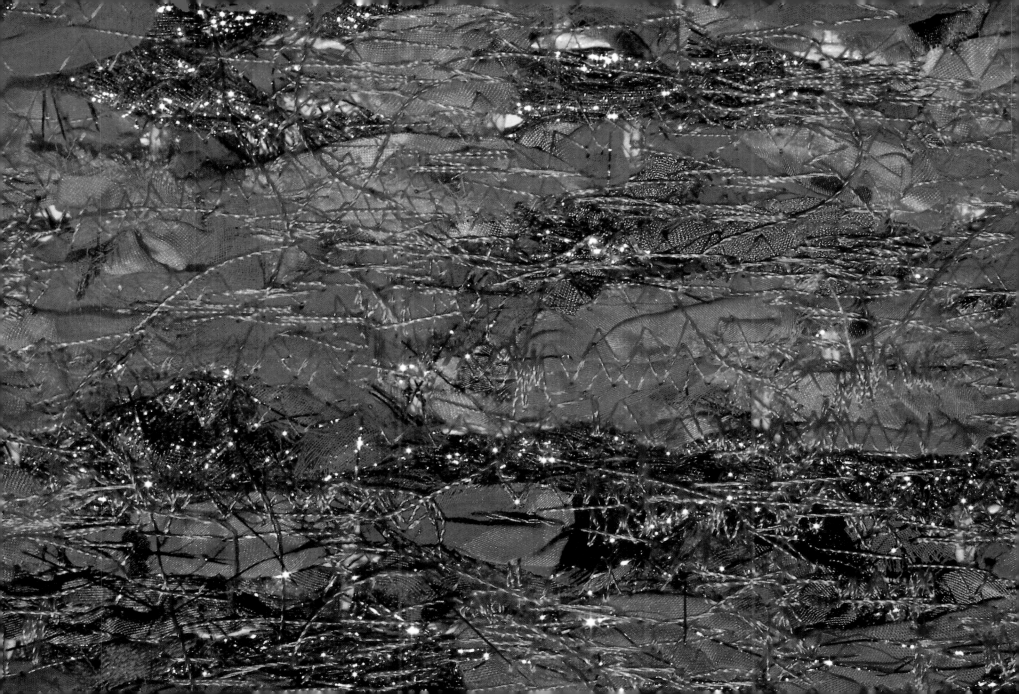

CHAPTER 4
Threads, Yarns and Textures

There was a time when anyone who suggested using anything other than Tapestry Wool, Crewel Wool or Tapestry Cotton for canvas embroidery was made to feel guilty of some unforgivable act. Happily those days are gone. For experimental work, as long as the thread will go through the canvas or can be couched on top, it can be used.

Today we have at our disposal a multitude of wonderful threads, those generally thought of as embroidery threads and many others besides; such as cottons, silks, rayons, hand-spun and hand-dyed wools, cottons and silks, ribbons, metallic cords and machine threads, knitting yarns, tapes, strips of fabric etc. Threads are available in a greater variety of colours and textures than ever before.

It is up to us to experiment with as many of these threads in as many variations and combinations as we can. Quite often the threads will take over and suggest new ideas as you work – one idea leads to another and before you know where you are you have produced an exciting new effect.

It is a good idea to delve into your left-over knitting yarns – or those of a friend. Keep the ribbons and ties used on gifts; take a new look at the trimmings on discarded garments; never throw anything away. It is even possible to extract threads from intricately woven braids and cords; never pass a 'bargain bin' without checking the contents for possible treasure.

Getting to know your threads and their potential is important, that is why it is good to work stitches on a variety of gauges of canvas with as many different threads as possible. Creating exciting textures is a basic feature of liberated canvas work. These textural happenings are produced by combining different types of thread and by exploiting the texture created by the stitches themselves. Be prepared to be inventive, mix different threads and colours together in the needle. Machine metallics and rayons are especially effective if 2 or 3 colours or shades, say from dark through to light, are mixed and gradually changed. Use fine thread on coarse canvas; thick, springy thread on a finer one; work the stitches larger or smaller; interchange the textures and make the work exciting.

SIMPLE WAYS OF DYEING THREADS...

Thread can be dyed quite easily in your own kitchen. This is a marvellous way to get exactly the effect you need. You can use up oddments of yarn which you would not otherwise use. I have several balls of very pale blue, mercerised knitting cotton which I will never use in its pale blue form. By dyeing it, however, I have an almost endless supply of new threads.

TRANSFER PAINT

Mercerised and stranded cotton, as well as synthetic yarns can be dyed with transfer paint. If you have coloured a piece of fabric or canvas by this method, try laying some thread, which has been wound off the ball, flat on the ironing board; then use the same piece of painted paper to iron off colour onto the thread. This will give you thread which is colour co-ordinated to match your canvas. Ideally the thread should be turned and colour transferred to both sides.

SILK PAINT

Tie thick threads into loose hanks; finer threads can be wound onto a plastic ruler. Wash the thread with soapy water and rinse well. Whilst still damp lay it in a glass dish – a large casserole or baking dish is ideal. Using a paint brush, dab colour direct from the pot onto the wet threads, leave for approximately 30 minutes so that the colour can be absorbed and then dry using a hair drier. Once the thread is completely dry it can be rinsed to remove excess dye and dried again either with the hair drier or by natural means. Some yarns accept dye more successfully than others and some not at all, so be prepared to experiment.

The small padded cushions in the picture on the right, were worked using combinations of machine rayon, single strands of stranded cotton and metallics to obtain the jewel like effect in the colours. These little cushions were backed with Thai silk to enhance the quality of rich colour and texture. Hung on handmade cords and suspended from wrapped dowels they form a mobile, but as individual cushions they make lovely chatelaines if a pair of embroidery scissors is attached to the cord at one end.

SPACE DYEING WITH COLD WATER DYES

The thread should be prepared as for silk paint dyeing but experiment with thread which has not been dampened. In addition to your shallow glass dish you will need some cold water dyes in powder form, a salt solution and a soda solution.

Mix 125 gms of cooking salt with 500 ml hot water and stir until completely dissolved.
Mix 125 gms household or washing soda with 500 ml hot water and stir until completely dissolved.
Mix ¼ teaspoon of dye powder with a tablespoonful of cold water, in a jam jar. Use a full teaspoonful of powder if a stronger colour is required. Add a little hot water to dissolve the powder thoroughly and then stir in approximately 200 ml of salt solution. Mix each colour in a separate jar.

Lay the dampened threads in the glass dish and gently spoon dye solution over them. Leave for at least 10 minutes to allow the colour to be absorbed and then *very gently and slowly* pour some soda solution over the threads until completely covered. Leave for a further 15 to 30 minues to fix the dye. Do not agitate the mixture at all during the dyeing process or the colours will mix. Wash threads in soapy water and rinse well. With practise and experimentation you should be able to produce some really creative threads. Remember though that this is an absorbing pastime and should not be attempted if you only have half an hour to spare, it is an all-day fun activity. Also make sure you have *lots* of thread prepared as it is quite addictive once you start, and a jam jar full of dye goes a long way! Once mixed the dye solutions will last for only a few hours.

In this piece, on the left, metallic ribbon was combined with rayon threads, mixed with machine metallics, as well as pearl cotton (Coton Perlé). In some areas the canvas is completely covered, whereas in others, it is seen through the stitches or even left unstitched altogether to create interesting textural contrasts. The full picture can be seen on page 58.

WRAPPING

Wrapping consists of neatly winding threads around a core. This core can be a piece of thin card, a plastic drinking straw, or a wooden dowel; it can also be a piece of string, thread or wire. The threads used to do the wrapping can be all one type or colour. Stripes and blocks can be formed by using different threads, both in colour and texture.

WRAPPED CARD

To wrap card, cut a thin piece of card to the required length, width or shape. Fold a piece of masking tape lengthwise down the centre, with the sticky side out, so that the tape can be stuck along the length of the card, but has a sticky side facing out as well. It is also possible to use double-sided tape. It is advisable to peel back the protective paper as you go, to avoid becoming 'stuck up'. The sticky side of the card is the back and is used to secure the end of the thread. Carefully cover the card by wrapping the threads as closely and evenly as possible. Make sure that the ends are securely attached – a clear fabric glue is best for the final ends; the others should be covered as the wrapping progresses. If several colours or types of thread are being used cut them into manageable lengths, or else a fine muddle, reminiscent of knitting with six balls of wool, will result. Wrapping a dowel would be done using the same method. Examples of wrapped card used as borders can be seen in the *Dandelion Garden* and the *Knot Garden* pictures on pages 50 and 52.

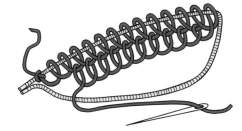

A wrapped wire can be bent to form a leaf shape and Buttonhole Filling used to complete the illusion, (See page 35).

The picture on the right shows examples of wrapping. From right to left: a hand-wrapped wooden dowel, a shaped card hand-wrapped, two different widths of wrapped card, a strip of machine-wrapped fabric, some hand-wrapped string, machine-wrapped string and machine-wrapped metallic thread.

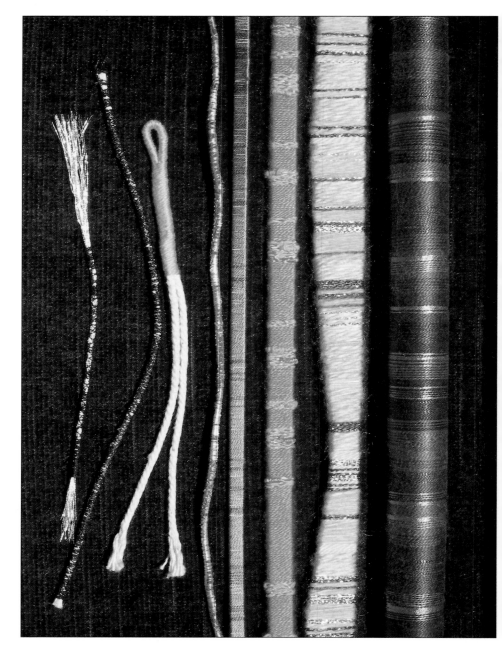

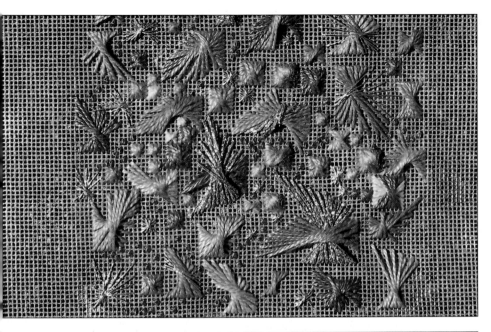

WRAPPED THREAD, STRING OR WIRE

By Hand — String

One method is to cut a piece of thread or string to the required length. Then using a slip knot, attach the wrapping thread to the top of the string with the tail hanging down so that it is covered as you wrap. Wind the thread evenly around the core until the desired length has been covered and secure with another slip knot. The end of the thread can be used to attach the wrapped thread to your work. The ends of the string can either be taken through to the reverse side of the work or, they could be frayed out, to form a tassel effect and coloured with paint or dye.

Another method is to cut a piece of string double the finished length required. Begin winding your wrapping thread around the string near the centre of the length, holding the loose end firmly (a small piece of 'magic' tape can be used to anchor it temporarily). When you have covered approximately 3 cm of the string, fold it in half to form a loop at the top and continue wrapping over both pieces of string. As with card, the wrapping can be done in any colour or texture of thread and changed to form patterns. When the string has been covered, thread the end of the wrapping thread back through the last few turns using a needle or secure with a slip knot as with the first method. Examples of wrapped string can be seen on pages 29, 40 and 62.

By Hand — Wire

Florist's wire and plastic-covered electrical wire can also be wrapped, using either of the methods mentioned above. Leaf and petal shapes can be formed by wrapping stranded cotton around florist's wire then working Buttonhole Filling inside the shapes as in the diagram opposite (page 34). The picture on page 57 shows a worked example. Covered wire leaf shapes can also be woven over in much the same way as making a Woven Picot. Some of the leaves on the border of *Marés Knot Garden* picture on page 51 were made in this way.

The picture top left was inspired by autumn leaves, and shows some interesting variations of Rhodes Stitch. The combination of pearl cotton (Coton Perlé), wool and fine metallic threads set against unstitched areas of canvas creates wonderful textural contrasts. *(By Pam May.)*

The experimental sample in the picture bottom left has produced some really striking textural effects, achieved by working Norwich Stitch in different sizes, some very large and even some oblong ones and by using combinations of wool, pearl cotton, and metallic threads. *(By Maré Abbot.)*

Machine Wrapping

String, strips of fabric, ribbon and wire can be wrapped using a sewing machine. To do this you will need to set your machine for machine embroidery or free machining: this entails lowering the feed dog or putting on a darning plate, depending on the type of machine. Remove the presser foot, insert a 90 or 100 needle and set the machine to work a wide zig-zag stitch. The upper tension will probably need to be looser than for normal stitching, it will depend on your machine, so be prepared to experiment. The stitch length should be set to '0'. Remember to lower the presser foot lever before you begin to stitch. Hold the string or wire firmly and tautly with both hands – one at the end of the string, beyond the needle the other just in front of the needle. Keep the string taut and feed it through the machine keeping it in the centre of the stitching plate, allowing the zig-zag stitch to wind around the string. Take care to keep your fingers clear of the needle. If using wire, do not let the needle hit the wire, as both will probably break. Beads can be threaded onto the wire before the wrapping is done and the wire wrapped between the beads – surprisingly the needle hops over the beads very effectively!

Pieces of wrapped braid or string can be incorporated in a piece of work to form fraying, a fringe or, as shown on the right, tree roots. The tree was made by first machine-wrapping a fairly thick string and then placing it onto painted and machined canvas. Further zig-zag was worked over the wrapped string and extra branches worked directly onto the canvas. The roots are machined-wrapped string joined together by holding them firmly and then allowing the machine to stitch in space until they become joined – not easy to explain but obvious once you try!

Right, a tree worked on rug canvas using machine-wrapped string.

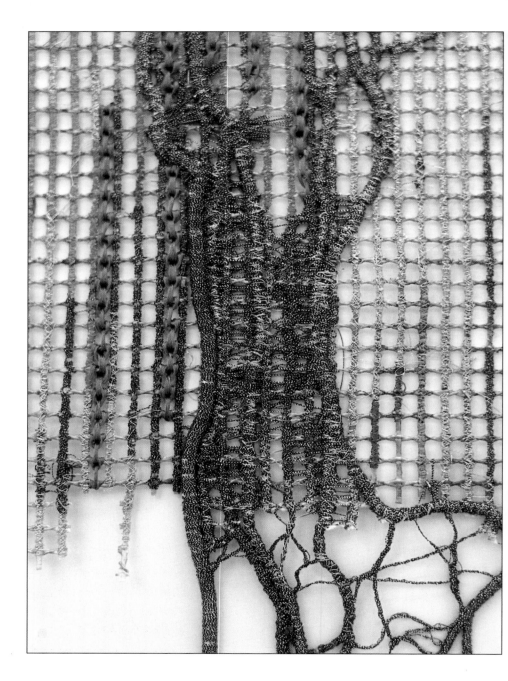

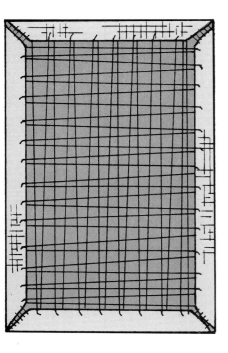

Method of lacing finished work over a board, before framing. The thread used for lacing must be strong enough not to snap when under tension.

If the work is to be finished as a hanging, a piece of interlining should be cut to the required finished size of the hanging, and the edges of the work turned over and stitched to it, using Herringbone Stitch.

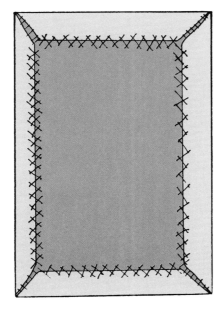

CHAPTER 5
Finishing Touches

There is a tendency to lose interest in a piece of work once the embroidery has been completed, but the finishing and presentation of your work is important. Samples and experimental pieces should all be mounted and filed, with notes and comments added for future reference. A light card with a 'window' cut in it is ideal: the sample is then placed face down onto the wrong side of the card with the embroidery seen through the 'window' and the edges secured with masking tape.

Pictures which are to be mounted and framed should be laced onto a board as shown in the diagram. It is advisable to consult your framer before deciding on the size of board as this could depend on the type of frame or whether you are going to have a mount. I would advise that you always lace or stretch your own work; many framers are not familiar with embroidery and often use glue, double-sided tape or spray adhesive instead of lacing; glue is death to your precious work as in time it discolours and can often be seen as ugly brown stains, so make sure it is never used. I would also suggest that in order to fully appreciate the wonderful textures which characterise liberated creative canvas work, you do not use glass when framing. However if you feel that you must use glass (and it does help to keep dust away), please use the clear variety as this does not deaden the work as is the case with so-called 'non-reflecting' glass. It is also important to ensure that the glass does not press down on the work: to avoid this you may need a to have a special boxed frame made.

If you have worked your embroidery on a frame it should not be distorted or require stretching into shape. In the event that it does need stretching, place a damp towel onto a wooden board and lay your embroidery on top. However, *do* make sure that any paint or dye used is colour-fast *before* you dampen any work! Also make sure that any fabrics or gauzes used will not be damaged by becoming damp. Because the work is likely to be highly textured it will need to be placed face up so as not to damage it. Pull the work into shape using drawing pins pushed through into the board and leave it to dry naturally. It can then be laced for framing or made up as required.

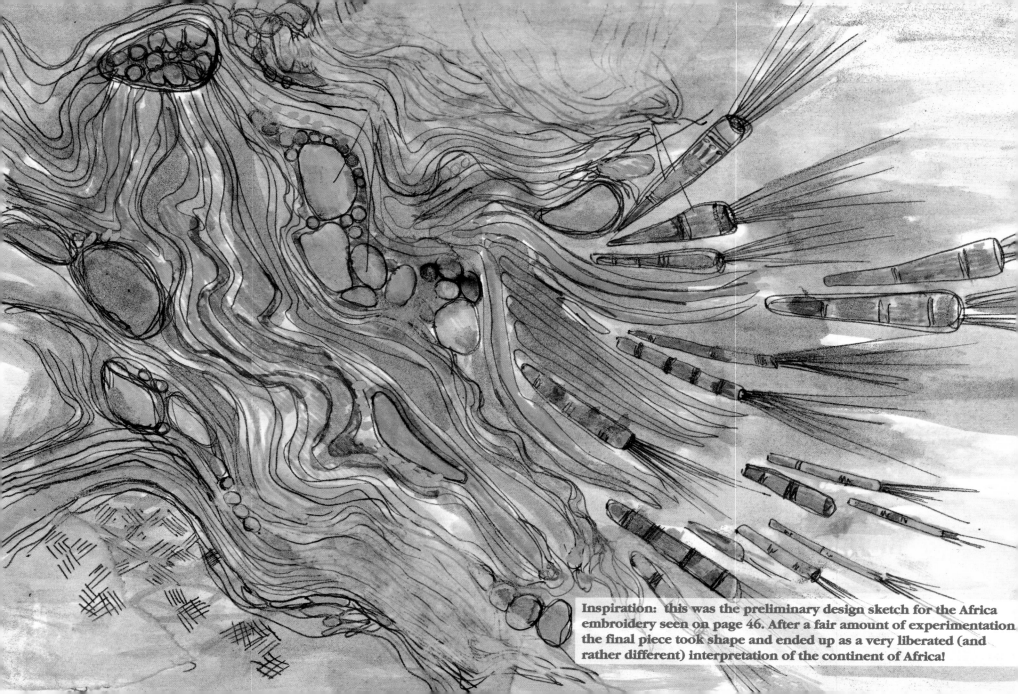

Inspiration: this was the preliminary design sketch for the Africa embroidery seen on page 46. After a fair amount of experimentation the final piece took shape and ended up as a very liberated (and rather different) interpretation of the continent of Africa!

The scrunched-up fabric and handmade wrapped beads which formed the initial inspiration for the map of Africa on page 46.

CHAPTER 6
Inspiration + Experimentation = Liberation

Once you have obtained a fair knowledge of a variety of stitches and have broken the initial barrier, allowing yourself to think laterally and to look for unusual effects and textures – both in embroidery and in what can be seen around you – you are ready to do some real experimentation. As can be seen from some of the work featured in this chapter, inspiration comes from many different sources. It may be from a scene viewed from a window, a photograph of flowers, or fallen leaves, textures or patterns seen on walls, tree trunks, or pathways, the tracks left by tyres in snow, sand or mud, wild gardens or formal gardens, a bundle of wonderful new threads, their contrasting textures and colours. So get into the habit of recording ideas and pictures, carry a notebook with you, look at the combinations of colour and patterns found in nature, take photographs, make photocopies of pictures seen in books or magazines, collect objects such as shells, feathers and driftwood which inspire you, keep a scrapbook and make your own reference files, but most of all, keep your eyes open. You will be surprised how much inspirational material there is all around you.

As it is so very important to work small experimental pieces before embarking on larger projects, several experimental samples are featured here before we study some finished works. The samples were worked in order to try out ideas, or to experiment with new techniques or stitches. Some of the stitch illustrations seen in Chapter 2 and samples in Chapter 3 were worked as experimental ideas. For example, the illustration showing Eyelets on page 17 was worked before embarking on the *Dandelion Garden* which can be found on Page 50.

It is sometimes thought that in order to be 'creative' all one needs to do is to 'break all the rules' – sometimes used as an excuse for not perfecting a technique. This is not the case: the rules can be broken or bent, but the fundamental technique must be learnt *first*, in order to fully exploit the possibilities and scope which the techniques offer. A good knowledge of the technique presents one with the freedom and ability to begin experimenting, and with experimentation comes liberation!

Experimental Samples

The more you experiment the more liberated and exciting your work will become. You will find yourself looking for new ways of doing things instead of accepting what has been done before. All these experimental pieces can, and should, be mounted on card and kept in a file as reference material. These form an invaluable source of ideas and inspiration for future projects. Even the pieces which you may consider 'failures' should be kept, so as to remind you what did not work and what not to do next time! It is neither possible nor desirable for everything that one produces to be 'useful' in the sense that it can hang on the wall or be made into a cushion or bag. Experimental exercises are *never* a waste of time or thread: they are a means of exploring new possibilities and cultivating ones creativity in a non-threatening way. They allow new techniques to be perfected and most of all they are fun!

This sample (opposite) illustrates a number of stitches and techniques. The gold lamé fabric has been applied over a piece of felt cut smaller than the lamé to suggest veins in a leaf. String has also been placed beneath the lamé and small stitches worked on either side to give a ridged effect. Another interesting feature is the Needleweaving emerging from inside pieces of wrapped plastic drinking straws. To wrap the straws, cut them into small pieces and place onto the canvas, then bring the needle up close to the straw on the inside and take the needle down again as close as possible on the outside, keeping the straw and the stitches upright, until it is completely covered. By placing several covered straws in groups, varying the height and thread used to cover them, some very interesting effects can be achieved. Knots and beads added at the base of the straws adds further texture. A good example of covered straws incorporated into a piece of work can be found in the detail of *Africa*, shown on page 47.
(This sample was later framed, and is now owned by Barrie and Jin Howard.)

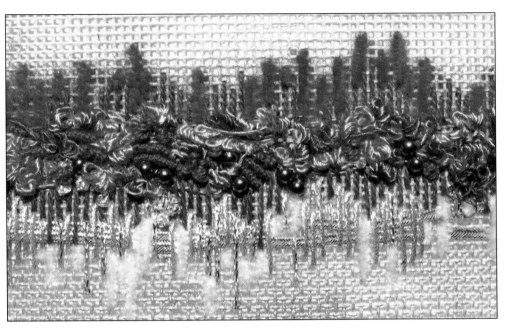

On the left is an exercise in couching. Pieces of silver Russia Braid have been couched down at the bottom, using long vertical stitches in metallic threads and chenille. The loopy knot-like area in the centre is a piece of novelty knitting yarn which is held in place with knots and beads.

Bottom left, was worked as a sample, where the canvas was dabbed with colour – gold fabric paint and pink drawing ink. The centre has long loose Bullion Knots and Bad French Knots worked in rayon and wool so that they remain springy. Long stitches worked in hand spun wool complement the Bullion Knots and the beads show off the French Knots.

Below, the sample was worked on canvas which had been coloured with gold fabric paint. The flower shape was formed by couching down a piece of Russia Braid, on edge rather than flat. Rice Stitches were scattered about, worked in knitting ribbon and rayon embroidery thread, with gold thread. The centre of the flower was built up using ruched gold ribbon and beads. To ruche the ribbon all you need to do is work a row of running stitches along the length of the ribbon and gather it up to the desired length: it can then be twisted and coiled to form interesting shapes. Strips of fabric can be ruched in the same way and, if desired, the edges can be left to fray out.

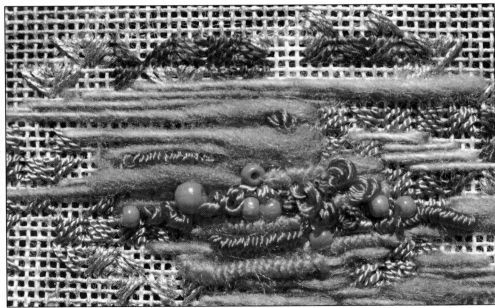

Right is a small sample, inspired by a flower-bed full of impatiens.

Below is an experimental piece which incorporates couched textured knitting yarn just below the Florentine stitched background. Cushion Stitch in a variety of thread thicknesses, together with French Knots, forms part of the foreground and Velvet Stitch bushes complete the impression of a small stitched landscape.

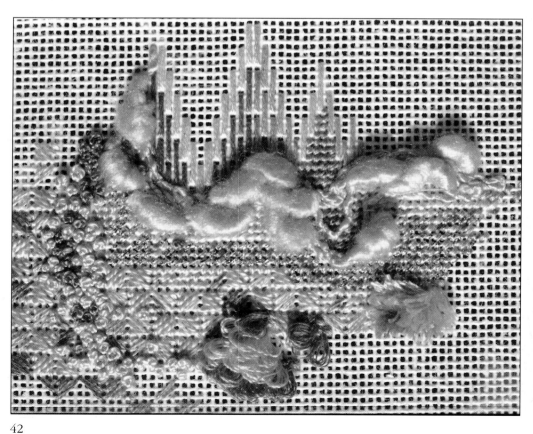

The picture on the left was worked on gold-painted canvas, this was an experiment in using metallic threads and unstitched areas of canvas, based on a Florentine theme.

The example below is free-flow Florentine where the colours and the threads have been allowed to take over and produce a vibrant and exciting effect. *(By Pam May.)*

The sample shown here was worked after making rough sketches from the patterns found on a shrivelled orchid leaf. String was laid on gold-painted canvas and horizontal stitches worked over it so as to cover the string and form ridges. The same method was used on the silver trees seen in the *Enchanted Forest* shown on pages 56 and 57. The spaces between the ridged areas were filled with knots and beads. The fringed ends of the string could also be painted, or taken through to the reverse side.

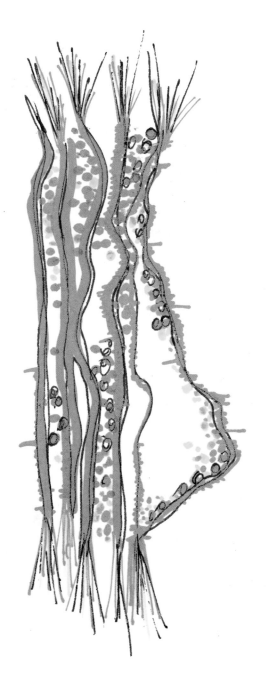

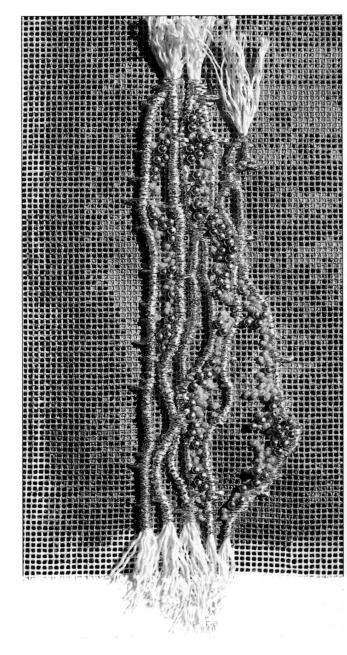

A sampler of borders worked in a variety of stitches and threads, is shown on the left. Rayon and metallic threads have been used together with stranded cotton, sometimes even in the same stitch. Stitches used include Rhodes, Herringbone, Cretan, Rice, Wheatsheaf, Crossed Cushion and Half Rhodes Stitch. *(By Luise Tyler.)*

Below is an experiment in interpreting a design (inset) found on a piece of printed fabric, using free Florentine Stitch. *(By Jennie Stock.)*

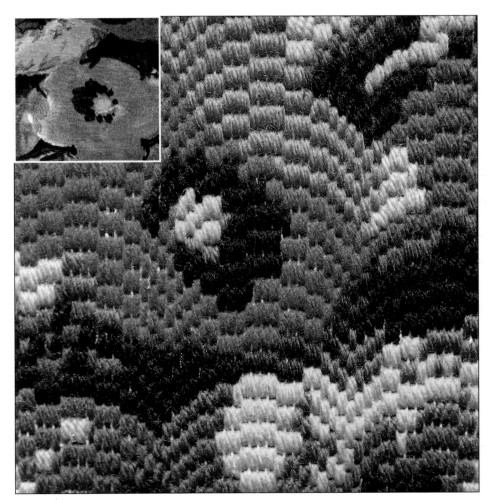

Finished Works

AFRICA *(owned by Mr Derek Gardner.)*

This is a perfect example of a piece of work not ending up as it started. I was inspired by a beautiful piece of scrunched fabric dyed in greens and gold – I even painted a design (see page 38) and made long hand-made beads from rolled paper, fabric and threads. I then dyed a length of fabric for the background and set forth with great enthusiasm, but the picture did not develop according to plan. The scrunched fabric did not seem to be compatible with the beads and the beads did not like the stuffed balls and French knots, and so it went on. So I left this project for a while at the end of my workroom, and stared at it in passing, until one day I decided to remove the beads and then the large piece of scrunched fabric and a couple of other dominating bits and pieces. What I was left with seemed to relax and look happier. I looked again and it seemed to resemble the bottom of Africa. Well that was it! I rushed off and scoured the atlases and eventually tacked the outline of Africa onto my fabric.

From then on it was all great fun and I stitched and stitched, added small pieces of painted canvas to the fabric and stitched some more until the inside of Africa was complete, comprised of stuffed fabric balls, beads, French and Bullion Knots, couched braid, wrapped wire, ruched fabric and ribbon, covered straws etc. Then I hit another snag. The dyed background fabric now seemed wrong for this highly textural piece of work, so after much deliberation I cut around Africa and applied it to a piece of canvas mounted on a frame and stitched a new background of Cushion Stitch, crossed in places with gold metallic thread. The textural balance was restored as was the colour tone and all was well at last. But one day I will have to come to terms with that piece of scrunched fabric and the handmade beads!

On page 47 – left is a detail of Africa, showing the rich textures of the work, which includes an applied canvas, beads, couched braid, scrunched fabric, knots and covered straws.

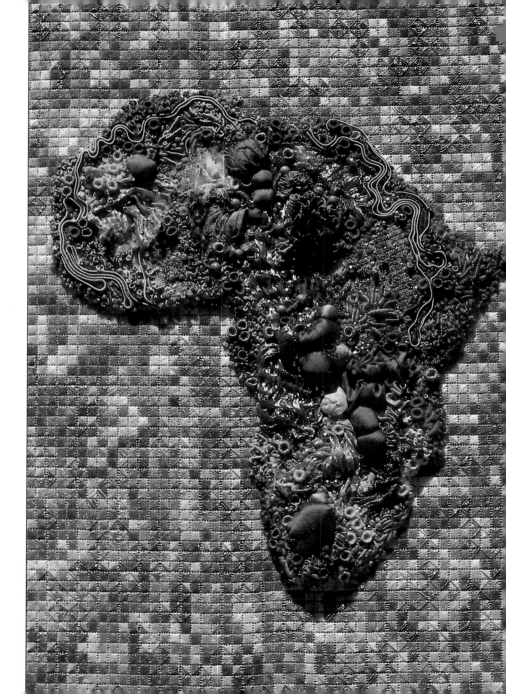

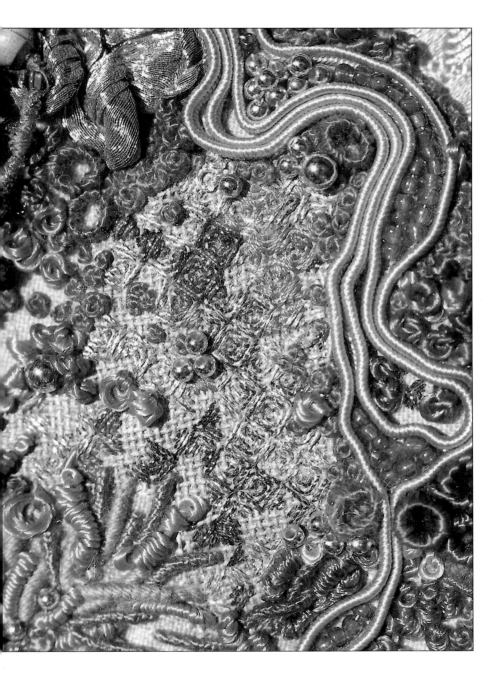

FLOWERS by Maré Abbott

The centre portion of this picture is worked entirely in Tent Stitch on a piece of painted canvas, using a variety of threads. In some places the canvas was left unstitched to add depth. The outer border has had threads withdrawn from the canvas allowing for Needleweaving to be worked over the remaining threads. A separate piece of canvas, stitched in Tent Stitch, was placed behind the main embroidery so that a stitched area is seen through the Needleweaving. Much of the charm of this little picture is the wonderfully vibrant use of colour.

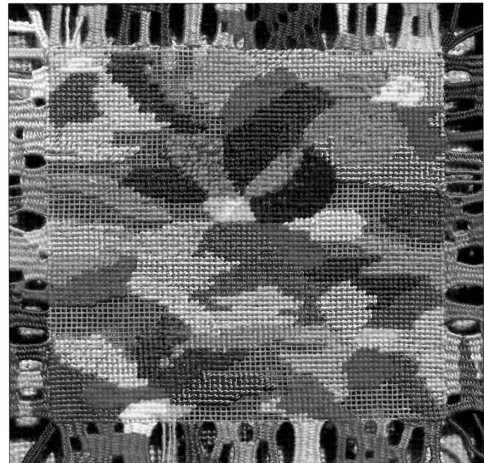

ARCHES

This picture was inspired by the view from a friend's studio window. I made a quick water-colour sketch and took some photographs so that the view, which so appealed to me, was recorded for future use. I tried a few ideas before the final one was chosen. I decided to work the arches themselves on a 22 gauge canvas covered with off-white silk. This allowed areas to be left unstitched so as to add to the brickwork effect. I worked with 2 shades of number 8 pearl cotton (Coton Perlé) in Cushion Stitch and Florentine Stitch. Once all the Canvas Work brickwork was complete it was removed from the frame. The canvas inside the archways was very carefully cut away, leaving sufficient canvas to turn in the edges. The silk was left so that it could cover the layer of fabric which was to be used for the next stage. A piece of lime green linen was mounted onto a frame and a piece of brown chiffon laid at the bottom to form the base of the foreground pathway. The Canvas Work arches were placed in position and tacked in place so that they would not move. Pieces of leather were cut out to represent the slices of tree trunk which formed the path. Finally the flowers, creepers and palm trees were worked using a great variety of threads. Note the French Knots, which were worked in all kinds of textures, from chunky hand spun wool and ribbon, to rayon embroidery thread and knitting ribbon.

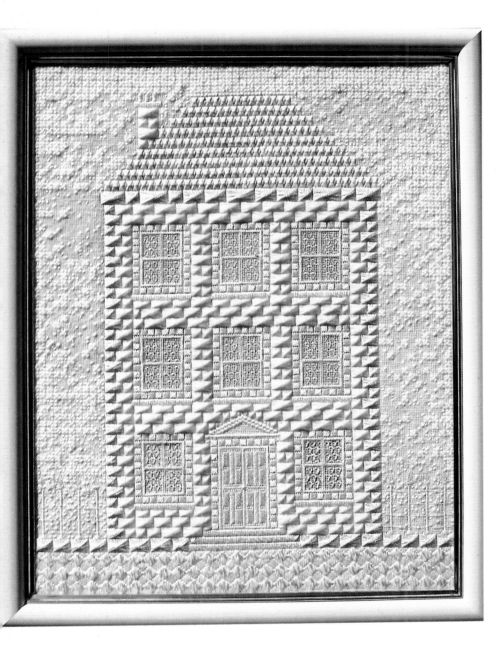

HOUSE

Worked on 18 gauge canvas, this monochromatic picture relies on the texture produced from the choice of stitches and threads. The roof is a variation of Wheatsheaf Stitch worked in tapestry cotton. The bricks of the house are worked in Rhodes Stitch, the outer ones in a pearl cotton (Coton Perlé) thread and the inner ones in an acrylic knitting yarn. About five different types of thread were tried before the ideal effect was achieved for the bricks which illustrates that one's first idea or choice is not always the one that works and that experimentation is essential.

The windows are first outlined in Cushion Stitch and then in Half Cross Stitch. The windows themselves also caused a problem as the first attempt – working them in Tent Stitch using a pearl cotton thread – was far too dense and heavy. It was only after some more experimenting that I discovered the solution: Wave Stitch. Pieces of shiny gold and silver fabric have been placed behind the windows and when the light shines on the work it twinkles through the unstitched areas, giving the impression that there are lights in some of the windows. The background is worked in Rice Stitch and Tent Stitch. The idea for this picture came from having worked a similar house in Hardanger. (I hope to do a Blackwork House too some day!) It was fascinating to find how different the two methods are, the totally different problems which needed solving – a very good learning process and an excellent exercise to attempt with any design.

DANDELION GARDEN

This picture was inspired by a trip to Europe in the spring. Everywhere I went there were fields of grass, dandelions, daisies and buttercups, and of course formal gardens. So the centre depicts the formal paths and paved areas of herb gardens bordered by low hedges, beyond is the wild meadow. This outer area is made up of random Eyelets worked in a variety of threads and the spaces between filled in with Half Cross Stitch. I used a selection of fine tapestry wool and rayon in several shades of green to achieve the background effect which is more interesting than if it had been stitched in only one colour or type of thread. The outer border is wrapped card.

This detail, of the picture on the right, shows the variety of stitches used in the formal garden, i.e. Wheatsheaf, Long-legged Cross, Brighton, Fan, Hungarian and Double Upright Cross Stitch.

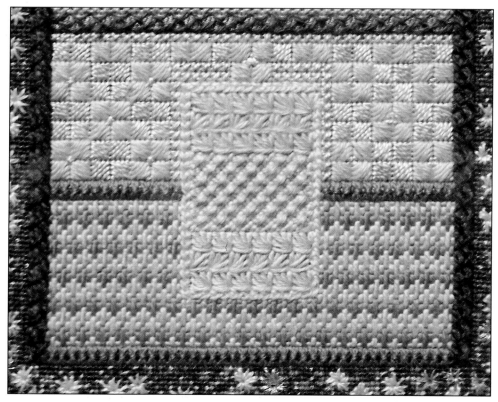

MARÉ'S KNOT GARDEN by Maré Abbott

The centre part of this picture was worked on linen, which was later applied to a piece of canvas and the Rice Stitch (over eight threads) border was worked onto the canvas. The flower border superimposed on the Rice Stitch is made up of Woven Picots, Bullion Knots, Detached Buttonhole Stitch Loops, Back Stitch Wheel (worked over beads) and wrapped string. This is another successful example of more than one technique being used in a piece of work.

The left-hand picture shows a detail of the border.

KNOT GARDEN

Inspired by pictures of formal Knot Gardens and Parterres, this 'Knot Garden' is really a Parterre – it has no looped 'knots' – and is worked on a heavy crash linen rather than on canvas. Nevertheless the paved areas of the garden are worked in Cushion Stitch and the gravel area in the centre in fine French Knots with a Backstitch Wheel in gold thread for the fountain. This picture illustrates the successful way in which canvas techniques can be used and combined with free-style embroidery. We see this combination again in *Arches* on page 48, in *Enchanted Forest* on page 56, and in *Marés Knot Garden* on page 51.

The hedges in this garden are couched metal thread; the formal flower beds are Bad French Knots in rayon thread, with small snippets of ribbon added. The meadow beyond is worked in random Eyelets and random Cross Stitch using only one strand of stranded cotton or silk. The inner frame or hedge is Raised Chain Band worked in knitting ribbon and the outer frame is No. 12 pearl cotton (Coton Perlé) thread and a fine gold thread wrapped over card.

Design sketch based on a 17th century parterre pattern.

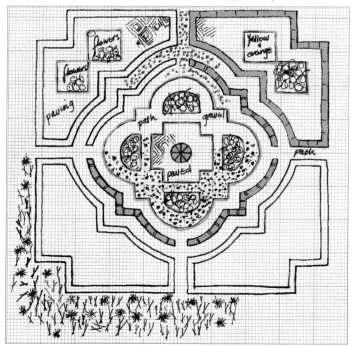

MISTY

This picture was inspired by a charted design in a book by Stafford Whiteaker called *English Garden Embroidery*. The grey cat was what caught my eye, but at the time I had a wonderful, much-loved black half Siamese cat, and she would have been very difficult to stitch. A few years later my black cat died and a new loveable grey feline entered my life and as she grew bigger I was reminded of the grey cat design. I am not disciplined enough to follow a chart, I admire those who can transpose all those dots and squares into intricate pictures in Cross Stitch or Tent Stitch, but my brain is not that ordered. After a frustrating attempt I decided to do my own thing. I copied the outline of the cat and sketched in the shaded areas – I drew this directly onto my canvas using a 3H pencil. I also wanted to experiment with putting a layer of organdie over my canvas and to stitch with fine machine thread, so I dyed a piece of white organdie with silk paint and laid it over the canvas. Before putting it onto a frame I sandwiched some small pieces of green chiffon between the organdie and the canvas, then machined around them to suggest the catmint in which Misty is sitting. When the canvas was mounted on a frame, I worked the cat in number No. 5 pearl cotton (Coton Perlé) thread in two shades of grey, using Tent Stitch.

Once the cat was finished I began on the background, experimenting with Norwich Stitch and Cushion Stitch worked in combinations of machine rayon and machine metallics, and every now and then a strand of stranded cotton. The border was formed by couching three rows of silver threads (couched in pairs) using two strands of stranded cotton and one piece of metallic machine thread in the needle at a time. The spacing of the couching stitches was varied to form a pattern. The outer border was machined to suggest a hedge and then loose, loopy Detached Chain Stitches and French Knots were added to give body and texture to the hedge. I hope that Mr Whiteaker approves of my version of his cat.

HANGING BASKET by Gretchen Reich

Inspired by the beautiful hanging baskets in Europe, Gretchen painted a picture from her photographs and then decided to stitch a hanging basket. The canvas was painted using fabric paint. The area behind the basket and flowers was machine stitched to represent a wall. The flowers are superimposed using random Cross Stitch, in other words, crosses which do not conform to the rules, and are irregular in shape and size.

The outer background area is Rice Stitch. The subtle colour changes have been so beautifully and successfully merged that they suggest dappled sunlight on a wall.

Right, Detail of flowers worked in random Cross Stitch, with beads added for extra textural effect.

Gretchen's painted design, which inspired her to stitch the Hanging Basket picture.

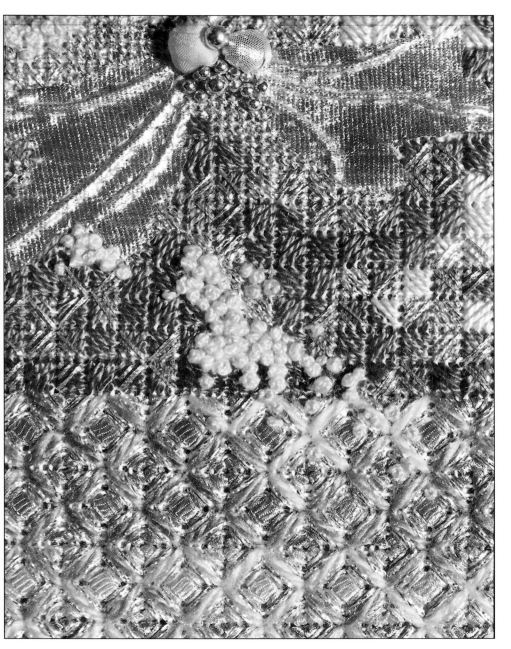

GILDED LILY

This piece started life as a small sample and, like Topsy, just grew. The centre portion was to illustrate the use of string placed under a gold fabric to suggest veins in the petals of a flower or leaf. The padded middle of the flower is made of small circles of fabric stuffed with cotton wool – this is done by cutting a circle of fabric, placing a row of running stitches around the edge, and pulling the thread up to close the opening. Before closing it completely, poke some cotton wool or wadding into the hole and secure the ends. The completed ball can then be attached to the work. At some stage I felt this little sample had potential, so I placed the small square of canvas onto another, larger piece of canvas – unfortunately not quite the same gauge, but after some fiddling I managed to cover the joins successfully. I worked four rows of Rice Stitch, over eight threads, around to form a border. The base crosses are worked in two different shades of knitting ribbon and the corners crossed using an acrylic knitting yarn, rayon machine threads and gold thread. By changing the tones of the corner stitches the border was made to change from predominantly green to gold. The French Knots, spilling out from the centre into the border, helped to integrate the outer and inner part of the work. When the embroidery was finished a piece of gold lamé fabric was machined around the edge to form an extra border before the work was framed.

ENCHANTED FOREST

Canvas work can form just part of a picture, as is seen here. The background base fabric was built up using scraps of fabric machined onto a calico base. Then a piece of machined, hand dyed muslin was added and both layers mounted onto a frame. The pieces of canvas were cut to shape and tacked into position. The stitching was worked through all the layers of fabric which meant that it was easier to work with a chenille or darning needle instead of the normal tapestry needle. Snippets of material and pieces of machine embroidery which had been worked on water-soluble fabric, were added to suggest foliage. Finally the foreground areas were worked. The wrapped wire leaves were made separately and then attached. The rocks were created by working Buttonhole Filling in thick wool over a shaped base. This base was made by dampening a piece of wine bottle sleeve (a sort of cardboard-maché material similar to that of an egg box) and moulding it into the desired shape by pinning it to a polystyrene tray (the kind veggies are packed in) and leaving it to dry.

This picture was the result of a challenge between a group of embroiderers: each was given a box of identical items, such as the muslin, small pieces of fabric, a piece of canvas, the wine bottle sleeve, florists wire, beads, seeds, feathers etc. Each person then had to create something using at least 75% of the items in the box, although we were allowed to add anything we liked. Quite a challenge, and a very good way to stretch the imagination!

GOLD AND PURPLE IMAGES

The inspiration for this piece came primarily from the threads themselves. I wanted to experiment with some newly acquired metallic ribbon as well as using rayon and metallic machine thread. The second idea was the desire to play with Cushion Stitch, Rice Stitch and unstitched areas of canvas. I began by working a small sample and then planned the layout on graph paper using felt-tipped pens and drawing inks, then I set off on the grand adventure. The canvas was mounted on a frame and painted using a gold fabric paint. I found that by working with different variations of threads within a theme of peacock colours and gold, some wonderful effects emerged. For example most of the Cushion Stitches are worked using two or three lengths of rayon machine thread and one or two lengths of metallic machine thread in the needle together – a total of four threads at a time. The large Rice Stitches are worked over eight threads of canvas using metallic ribbon for the base cross, with finer threads worked on top. Small squares of purple and gold leather were added, held down by the Cushion Stitches. Once all the stitching was complete the edges of the canvas were cut, following the pattern outline made by the stitches. The canvas was mounted onto a piece of gold card using invisible nylon thread, before being framed. See page 33 for detail.

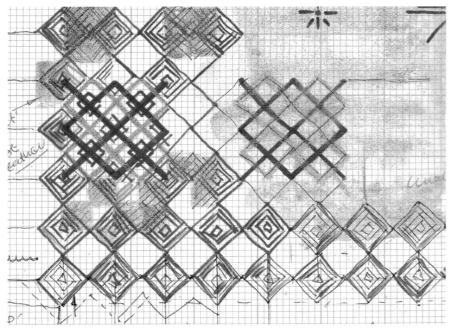

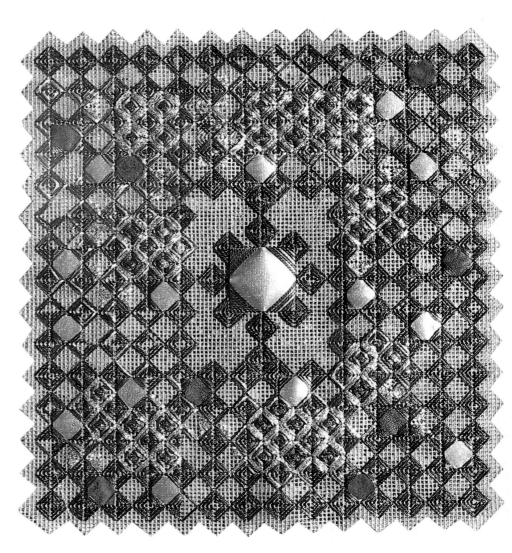

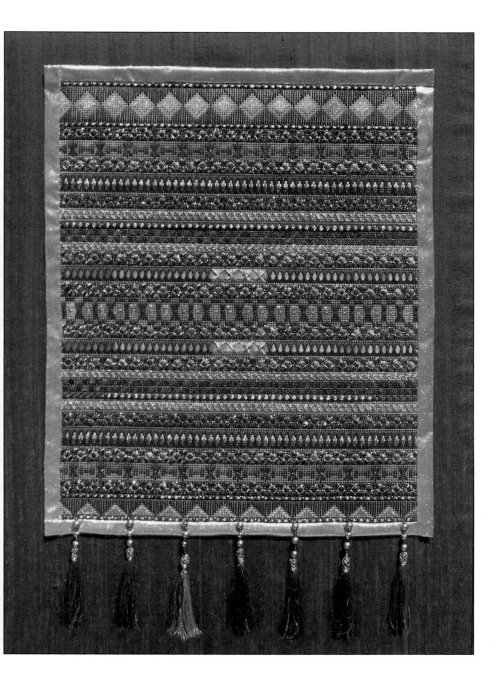

A PURPLE POUCH

Here we have borders of stitches worked to form an overall pattern. The initial sample was worked on a piece of canvas coloured with pink drawing ink, and stitches were used to form borders and patterns. Variations of Wheatsheaf Stitch were used as well as Rice Stitch and a Cross Stitch variation ("Penny's Cross") where the cross was worked over 3 vertical threads and 4 (later 2, 3 or even 6) horizontal threads; a second cross was worked into the remaining holes, as shown in the diagram below. The small crosses were worked over narrow ribbon, whilst wider ribbon was threaded through the larger crosses. What started as a little sample was later edged with gold lamé fabric, padded, lined with Thai silk and embellished with tassels, to form the Purple Pouch which is seen below.

BORDERS AND BEYOND

This illustrates admirably how the working of samples and experimenting can lead to a large, successful piece of work. The picture (left) resulted from a development of the small sample mentioned above, using the same basic idea, but with a larger variety of threads and stitches – especially Penny's Cross – this piece just evolved!

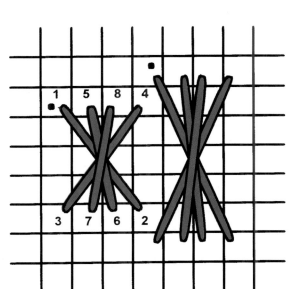

SUMMER GARDEN

Inspired by a photograph in a book on gardens, this piece is worked on 14 gauge canvas which was first coloured using water-soluble pencils to suggest the various areas of colour. The source picture had three different types of flowers in it, so I decided to treat each in a different way. The yellow ones are worked in Rice Stitch and Cross Stitch, the purple ones in looped Velvet Stitch, and the orange ones are tufts of chiffon and dyed medical gauze. The foliage is worked in random Cross Stitch and Cushion Stitch using many different types of thread, including strips of fabric like chiffon and muslin. Remember, when stitching with strips of fabric, you need to cut the fabric on the bias or it will disintegrate as you work! It is best to work with short lengths.

INFINITY by Tricia Elvin-Jensen

As a result of attending one of my Creative Canvas Work courses, this embroiderer began experimenting with Rice Stitch and became so involved with it she decided to concentrate solely on what she could do with Rice Stitch. The canvas was painted and a great many different threads used. The stitch has been really exploited to form some lovely textured areas. The wrapped portion was worked over a piece of card cut to the desired shape, then attached to the main piece of work. A silver fabric edging glue was used to seal the cut edge of the canvas and the loose canvas was mounted on a padded block so that it became a three dimensional piece. Strong nylon fishing line was threaded through some knitting ribbon and then ruched to form the free-standing curves.

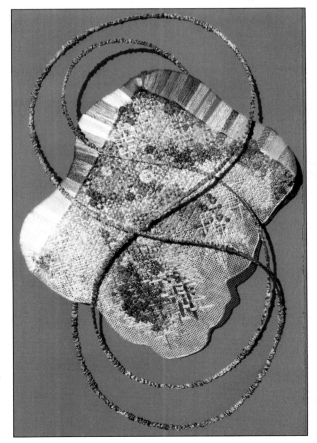

EXPERIMENTAL PIECE by Jutta Farringer

In this experimental piece of work the embroiderer has incorporated as many as six different gauges of canvas thus allowing a greater variety and scope for stitches and threads to be used. The various small pieces of canvas (mostly off-cuts) were stitched together using a zig-zag machine stitch and the resulting larger composite piece coloured using fabric paint. The use of the paint gave a continuity to the work and allowed areas to be left unstitched. A wonderful variety of yarns was used to develop the interesting textures. The actual number of stitches used is not large, but because of the varying gauges of canvas they appear very different. The work also incorporates hand and machine wrapped threads and ruched chiffon. The inspiration for this piece of work came from the challenge of using different sizes of canvas and as many different types of thread as possible while attending a course on Creative Canvas Work. Another detail of this picture can be seen on page 11.

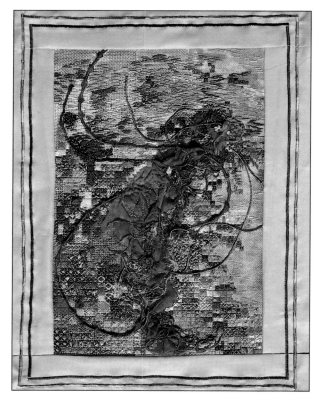

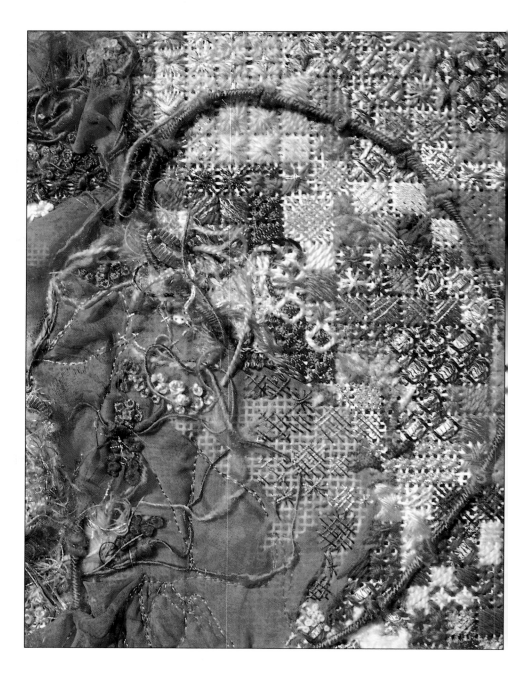

TOODY'S GARDEN by Toody Mouton

Toody's liberated garden is worked on a canvas which was first dabbed with fabric paint. A small picture of a garden taken from a magazine was the source and a one-day workshop with Vicky Lugg provided the initial inspiration. The result is a wonderful impressionistic interpretation of a summer garden. The success of this piece of work is due mainly to the use of only a few stitches and a clever variety of fine threads in well chosen colours. These allow the painted canvas to become part of the picture. The stitches used are variations of Rice Stitch, Cushion Stitch and Cross Stitch together with French Knots and Eyelets. This was the first piece of free, creative canvas work that this embroiderer had worked!

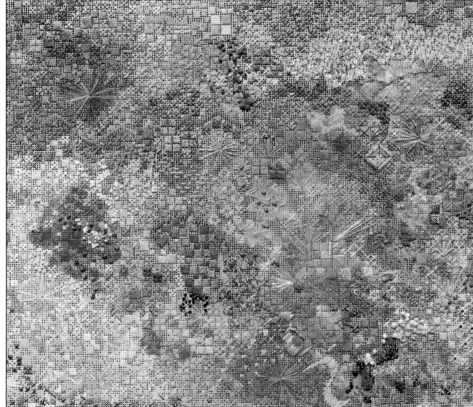

FURTHER READING...

Title	Author	Publisher
The Good Housekeeping book of Needlepoint		Ebury Press
The Madeira Book of Needlepoint Stitches	Susan Higginson	Madeira Threads
Stitches on Canvas	Mabel Huggins & Clarice Blakey	Batsford
Dictionary of Canvas Work Stitches	Mary Rhodes	Batsford
Working on Canvas	Margaret Rivers	Batsford
Embroiderer's Workbook	Jan Messent	Batsford
Canvas Embroidery	Peggy Field & June Linsley	Meerhurst/Delos
Needlepoint	Mary Rhodes	Octopus
Needleweaving	Edith John	Batsford
Fabric Painting for Embroidery	Valerie Campbell-Harding	Batsford
Machine Embroidery – Stitch Techniques	Valerie Campbell-Harding & Pam Watts	Batsford
English Garden Embroidery	Stafford Whiteaker	Century
Embroiderer's Garden	Thomasina Beck	David & Charles

Other books published by Triple T Publishing c.c.
SATIN & SILK RIBBON EMBROIDERY by Lesley Turpin Delport ISBN 0-620-17755-1
JUST FLOWERS by Lesley Turpin Delport ISBN 0-958-38733-8
TWO CUSHIONS AND A QUILT by Sue Akerman ISBN 0-958-38731-1

Triple T Publishing c.c.
29 Colenso Road Claremont 7700 Cape Town, South Africa.
Fax +27 21 61-7746